Puliziotta's Organizational Health and Fitness

Lessons Learned and Strategies for Zapping the DYSfunctional Virus

Emma Kowalenko

(handwritten inscription): To Ben you and your museum for people w/ disabilities! Emma

Library of Congress Control Number: 2016908144
CreateSpace Independent Publishing Platform, North Charleston, SC
ISBN-13: 978-1533234704
ISBN-10: 1533234701
Cover and Photos for Graphics by Emma Kowalenko
Puliziotta Images and Text™

DEDICATION

I dedicate this book to two women who make up a good part of the fabric of my being; my grandmother and my mother. Emma Esther Kalmus Podrobnik, whose soul was extinguished by World War II's holocaust, never fulfilled her dream of writing a novel. Eugenia Genendla Podrobnik Kowalenko reigned as cleaning lady supreme in the maternity ward of Norwegian American Hospital in Chicago, between the years of 1968 and 1985.

CONTENTS

Aristotle said:

"Educating the mind without educating the heart is no education at all."

Leonardo da Vinci said:

"It had long since come to my attention that people of accomplishment rarely sat back and let things happen to them. They went out and happened to things."

Picasso said:

"If you want to paint, close your eyes and sing a song."

ACKNOWLEDGMENTS

A huge thank you to my dear husband and life partner, Anthony Bilotti, whose support of my creative and professional endeavors has made the production of this book less daunting. Thank you to my ever encouraging sons Adrian and Jonathan. I am grateful to Judith Kaufmann and Stan Lester for their wisdom and dedication to editing text and sources. I thank a friend who wishes to remain anonymous for her meticulous research and editorial skills and artistic handcrafts. The earrings she made inspired Puliziotta's all-seeing owls. I thank my art mentor and teacher Cheryl Steiger for standing by my innumerable changes to the illustrations in this book. Heartfelt thank yous to Laurie Kahn and Mary Jane Gabrielsen, fellow writers who so generously found time to spend coffee shop musings in comradeship. With gratitude I acknowledge the inspiration of the Mindfulness Based Stress Reduction (MBSR) teachings by Christopher Chroniak of the Insight Center in Chicago. Thank you to Kevin Croke, Dean Emeritus at the University of Illinois School of Public Health and Raymond Krizek, Stanley F. Pepper Professor and Director of the Civil and Environmental Engineering Department at Northwestern University's McCormick School. Thank you to Lean Construction mentor and practitioner, Rich Seiler, Chief Improvement Officer at Unified Works, Al Heystek, Licensed Professional Counselor, and Edward Kaufman, MSE, LCSW, BCD, for their reviews. Though I cannot share the names of clients to whom our company has been providing consulting services since 1988, I want to acknowledge and thank all the dedicated individuals with whom I have had, and continue to have, the pleasure of working. I am indebted to private, public, nonprofit sector leaders at all levels who continue to gift me with their expertise. Thank you to my readers. Together with you, we go beyond case studies. We visit and interact with real people pursuing solutions in real situations.

INTRODUCTION

On this journey author and protagonist greet you with a blended voice. I have written this guide as environmental planning company owner, change management consultant, and poet. Stress and related ailments from unhealthy physical or remote work environments, lack of work life balance, pose serious public health risks. I attribute these to the DYSfunctional virus* (DYS). My personal and professional life experiences prompt me to combat DYS at work with the purpose of attaining and maintaining *Organizational Health and Fitness* (OH&F). My protagonist Puliziotta, entered my creative sphere and mindfully* re-minded me that my mission needs her. And, no question, it does. You'll find out as I have, that you want to have Puliziotta on your team.

Please note that an asterisk after a word when it first occurs in the text means the word or phrase will appear in the "What We Mean When We Say…" section following this introduction.

Puliziotta's name is a play on words in Italian. Flip the vowels, "o" and "u" and you have poliziotta a female detective, and puliziotta a cleaning lady. Why Italian? Why not? From signature bandana to metaphorical investigative tools, cleaning equipment and applications (apps) with super powers, this cleaning lady / detective persona fits the creatively practical thrust of this book. Together we zap* DYS. Using metaphors, mindfulness, and emotional, social, and cultural intelligence – EQ, SQ, CQ*, we transform our work environments.

Puliziotta embodies my personal and professional roots. As new immigrants in the U.S., my mother and I cleaned offices. Higher education and professional experience enabled me to establish my environmental and strategic planning firm in 1988. Puliziotta approaches cleaning up DYS contaminated workplaces as our company does environmental assessments and remediation projects; in phases, with a CORE* team.

Multi-cultural, multilingual, and multi-disciplinary describe me well. Born in Morocco to Eastern European parents, immigrating to the United States at the age of 11, life circumstances gifted me with several foreign languages. My diverse educational and professional backgrounds give me the skills to identify challenges and implement solutions. My entrepreneurial spirit gives me the creative hutzpah to make things happen.

Our company's private, public, and nonprofit sector clients run the gamut in terms of size and workplace environments, virtual and physical. My professional career as employee, employer, and consultant provide the basis for the five working lives presented here.

I strongly believe that sound and lasting *OH&F* can make ours a better world to work in and live in. Hop on as Puliziotta gives wings to our voyage. After laying down basic precepts, let's explore five distinct work environments through our mindful*, problem-solving lens.

Together with you, we travel, learn; lead the charge against toxic DYS invasions. We take mindful breaks to focus. We re-learn to play, write poetry and prose, draw, and take deep healthful breaths, practice yoga, listen, and see, with mind and heart. We brainstorm, gamestorm, and taste every bite of life's lessons. With mindfulness* we differentiate between information and wisdom. We heed lessons from nature, geese flying in V formation taking turns at leading the group. We incorporate adaptive leadership* into our decisions and actions.

We celebrate diversity. We discern between expected and unexpected changes and adapt our change preparedness responses accordingly. We accept the inevitability of natural and people created imbalance and move on to change management. Our tools find information quickly. With data we transform knowledge into wisdom.

INTRODUCTION

You dear reader, Puliziotta, and I, represent the "we" on this journey. Rules of the game for us are integrity, honesty, trust, and respect. These pillars form our foundation for taking on the challenges of eliminating DYS. With clear vision, practicality and creativity, together, we customize solutions to eliminate toxic behaviors caused by DYS. We create healthy work environments to make a difference for colleagues, friends, family, and ourselves.

Puliziotta and I share the passion for creating a healthy working world. Our active mindfulness approach builds leadership skills with the interface and the multilingualism of EQ, SQ, and CQ. We infuse antidotes to transform DYSfunctional toxicity into vitality. We engage our full individual and collective brain power* to zap unhealthful behaviors.

Puliziotta responds to calls seeking balance. In her gutsy, no nonsense way she dedicates her energies to discovering and blocking DYS from undermining *OH&F*. Her metaphorical cleaning, health measuring, and body building tools clear paths toward long term solutions. Lasting *OH&F* depends on our leadership skills to pursue ongoing discovery, to persevere with action. Action, a key word in transforming, top down, bottom up, across, and out of, static, boxed up " we've always done it this way," mindsets. To meet our goals of discovering lasting DYS antidotes we create a "land of do and does" built on self-awareness, rich with nutrients for fostering dynamic fully engaged brains. We are proudly multilingual. We speak and understand the languages of mindfulness, relationships, and cultures.

In commuter train, car, on foot, on a bike, plane, taxi, train, on metaphorical wings, on a magic carpet; pick your locomotion, your kinetic energy. Together we blaze the trail toward sustainable *OH&F*. We want to maintain *OH&F* for the betterment of society. A lofty goal? You bet. Doable, of course! Let's escort DYS out of our working lives.

No luggage needed to embark on this adventure. Grab your life experience, creativity, and self-confidence. Off we go with Puliziotta!

What We Mean When We Say "..." Our Glossary

<u>Adaptive Leadership</u> – We incorporate change management methods such as those described by Ron Heifetz and Marty Linsky with leadership skills that adapt to resolve unpredictable changes.

<u>CORE Team</u> – It takes a team to discover and zap the DYSfunctional Virus (DYS) with Collaboration, Optimism, Resilience, and Excellence.

<u>DYSfunctional Virus (DYS)</u> – Source of contamination and imbalance for working lives, day to day operations, and infrastructure DYS negatively affects the triple bottom line of people, planet, profit.

<u>Emotional Intelligence (EQ), Social Intelligence (SQ), and Cultural Intelligence (EQ), their Interface and Multilingualism</u> – With EQ we grasp what makes us and others human. With SQ we hone the capacity to understand relationships. With CQ we distill universal behaviors, those specific to a group, and those neither specific nor universal.

<u>Full Brain Thinking</u> – Tapping into our full brain's capacity with EQ, SQ, and CQ maximizes our individual and collective full brain power.

<u>Lean Management</u> – Managing by respecting people's talent and time. Not squandering the most precious resource; people energy as pioneered by Dr. Jeffrey K. Liker in the *Toyota Way*.

<u>Mindfulness Practice</u> – Since its introduction in 1965 by Jon Kabat-Zinn, scientific studies have validated the benefits of mindfulness practice on enhancing EQ, SQ, and CQ leadership competencies.

<u>*Organizational Health and Fitness (OH&F)*</u> – The essence of our mission, essential for public health and for an improved world to work and live in. We want to transform working environments for the long term.

<u>Zap</u> – With experience, creativity, knowledge, and wisdom, we zap, switch the channel from toxic behaviors filling our workplace ecosphere to sustainable environments free of contamination.

1   PULIZIOTTA'S WELCOME

Welcome to this first in a series of *Organizational Health and Fitness –* *(OH&F)* journeys. Mindfully aware and present in the now of each working person's life and workplace situation we use our engaged full brain, emotional intelligence (EQ), social intelligence (SQ), and cultural intelligence (CQ), to

Observe   Listen   Learn   Resolve.

I am Puliziotta, Chief Zapping Agent (CZA). I operate "undercover" as a cleaning lady. I am partial to bandanas, metaphors, all- knowing owls, infographics, and tools with traditional as well as high-tech powers. I mean business when it comes to zapping DYS.   The root of my name, Puliziotta, the Italian verb "pulire," means "to clean." Calling on engaged, full brain, capabilities I invite you to create a better world to work and live in by eradicating the DYS virus that threatens working people in all sectors of the global economy. I founded Zappers, ULTD, specialists in DYS cleanup, prevention, and workplace transformation. I welcome you to travel with me responding to calls to our Zappers DYSpatch Emergency Response (ER) Center. You are here because you care and want to tackle DYS. Together, with sound body, mind, and spirit, we undertake our mission to improve working lives.

During our travels we interweave reality with humor and hard work. The walls have ears and statistics tap their way to our actively mindful, engaged full brain, consciousness. We take along watchful owl eyes mobile apps, investigative tools, and of course, cleaning supplies. We scan data clouds for information and engage teams dedicated to Collaboration, Optimism, Resilience, Excellence (CORE).

With each work place challenge we encounter, we establish a CORE team. We exchange knowledge. We share our individual stories. We mindfully listen to others, to their individual and their collective stories. Your solutions will come from you and your CORE team.

Your CORE Team
Restores Organizational Balance through

Collaboration, **O**ptimism, **R**esilience, and **E**xcellence

Our mission succeeds when we form, find, and join CORE teams. No one can or should combat DYS alone. Your CORE team zaps and transforms physical and remote working environments.

 Mindfulness – Re-Minder

The success of each DYS zapping mission, to remove DYS and transform our physical and remote working environments depends on the perseverance of our CORE team and the strength of our building blocks.

Our *OH&F* Building Blocks and Keystone

We nurture the resources necessary for *OH&F* building blocks and keystone for a nurturing, positive landscape.

You and your CORE team call on your collective engaged full brain power.

- Describe a welcoming work place landscape.
- What building blocks would you include?
- What is your keystone?
- Chart your transformation timeline.
- Tell your individual and collective stories
- Construct your pillars, your landscape, and your building blocks.

Our journey includes a hands on work week during which we bring into awareness the working lives of five Very Important Persons (VIPS) at five workplaces with distinct DYS challenges. Understandably, the names of organizations or individuals whose daily work lives we visit have been changed. You may recognize someone, or even see yourself in our tool kit's MagnifEye Mirror. Together we identify DYS. With your input we create fitting resolutions for each case study.

Monday – IT Guru Mr. Unheard-Overworked (Mr. U.) at the Professional Design and Construction, Co. (PDC), a medium sized, privately owned firm, with 65 employees.

Tuesday – Accounts Payable Maven Ms. Trustworthy-Frustrated (Ms. T.) At Accounts Payable Department (APD), 12 employees, within the Primary Accounting Division (PAD), of 32 employees, all within the Municipal Public Agency (MPA), totaling 547 employees.

Wednesday – Competitive Spirit Ms. Insecure-Climber (Ms. I.) at Small Business Lending Section (SBL), seven employees, within the Business Lending Department (BLD), 16 employees, in one of three branches of Your Community Bank (YCB, N.A.), 42 employees. We meet Ms. I after the purchase of YCB by a national bank of 18,700 employees.

Thursday – Office Glue Extraordinaire, Executive Administrator, Mr. Loyal-Unappreciated (Mr. L), manages a U.S. office of an international nonprofit, social service agency, four employees, 5-15 volunteers depending on need and events. Top Education for All (TEFA), provides access to education for underserved urban populations. Based in Geneva Switzerland, TEFA has 20 international locations, 125 employees, 75-100 volunteers.

Friday – Entrepreneur Supreme, Mr. Captain-Misguided (Mr. C.) owner, CEO, CFO, boss, of family-owned Creative Print Marketing, Inc. (CPM), 38 employees.

2   WHY, WHAT, HOW, WHO

We map our journey from four perspectives – aerial, on the ground, third eye, and in person. These converge at destination; long term *OH&F*. Viewed from four perspectives all roads lead to *OH&F*.

- The **aerial perspective** relates to the **why** that delineates our purpose, our social responsibility. We are dedicated to creating a healthy working world. We use statistics as resources and backdrop, for tackling the DYS challenges in our work environments. We go beyond information to get at the cause. Einstein famously said "information is not knowledge; the only source of knowledge is experience." We thrive on experience.

- The **on the ground** perspective presents the **what**; our methodology for our investigations. This details our approaches, and tools. This perspective defines symptoms, and information gathered. On the ground, we assess the characteristics of the DYS infection. We mindfully draw on our experience and observations. These lead to knowledge which leads to specific actions for preventive measures.

- The **third eye**, the mindful perspective, the **how** leads to transformative solutions customized for each *OH&F* challenge. Life experience, multi-disciplinary expertise, and realistic expectations guide us in zapping DYS and implementing dynamic, realistic, and effective action plans.

- The **in person eye**, the direct person to person communication, the **who**; the CORE team that implements the solutions engaging full brain thinking competencies, in a knowledgeable, empathetic, sensible, EQ, SQ, CQ way.

Why this Journey? We take seriously our social responsibility to make this a balanced, healthy, and fit world to work and live in; our individual and group *OH&F*. Our efforts bring benefits to public health. We address work related stress, talent retention, employee engagement, customer and constituent satisfaction, and the triple bottom line of people, planet and profit.

The healthiest companies bring the best financial returns. The *Organizational Health: The Ultimate Competitive Advantage*, McKinsey Quarterly Article, June 2011, states, "To sustain high performance, organizations must build the capacity to learn and keep changing over time." The article continues, "Getting and staying healthy involves tending to the people-oriented aspects of leading an organization, so it may sound 'fluffy' to hard-nosed executives raised on managing by the numbers. But make no mistake: cultivating health is hard work."

The McKinsey & Company Report of 2014 entitled *"The Hidden Value of Organizational Health"* says, "When we compared the health metrics of more than 270 publicly traded companies with their financial-performance metrics, we found that the healthiest generated total returns to shareholders that were three times higher than those of companies in the bottom quartile and over 60 percent higher than those of companies with 'middle of the road' health profiles. We have not yet isolated the specific health effect for the sample as a whole, but judged by the energy and insurance-company examples, it is likely to be substantial." Conclusion: raise the organizational health profile.

What is *OH&F*? Trust, resilience, ethics, and fairness coursing through the veins of an organization result in *OH&F* evidenced by a strong heartbeat and a steady pulse. Leadership at all levels must take stress prevention seriously. Providing opportunities for employees to practice active mindfulness further enhances *OH&F*. Commitment and policies dedicated to career growth and welfare of each employee sustain a high *OH&F* index.

> **What is DYS?**

DYS an opportunistic virus infiltrates voids. It takes advantage of imbalance caused by change. It infects the workplace with harmful behaviors. DYS thrives during leadership transitions interjecting confusion, insecurity, and stress. It gums up smooth structural workings by masking existing strengths. DYS can slip in subtly or hit with gale-force winds.

> **How DYS Affects *OH&F***

DYS infects people at all levels. It insidiously alters response to change. Loyal employees when faced with situations for which they feel unprepared lose loyalty if they experience insecurity and stress. Lack of control can result in a fight or flight mode with symptoms of casting blame on others, and becoming punitive and rude. We cannot afford the loss of loyalty. It is a hard earned treasure. Loyalty sustains private, public, or nonprofit entities in good and hard times.

> **Who Detects and Zaps DYS?**

Together as a CORE team we follow a four step research, analysis, cleanup, and restoration to equilibrium method. With the right tools we detect the structural gaps, leadership voids, and resilience weaknesses. We conduct holistic Strength, Weakness, Opportunities, Threats (SWOT) analyses. Holistic because we go beyond SWOT data. We account for subjectivity in findings, prioritize actions, and implement workable, realistic, customized solutions.

> **Who Cures DYS?**

A dedicated CORE team removes underlying causes for DYS by implementing mindful action plans appropriate for each situation. We prioritize our cleanup by severity of the infection. The five working environments and working lives we explore during this journey illustrate DYS encroachment, eradication, cures, and preventive measures. For sustained *OH&F*, we build on strengths. We communicate mindfully. We use the lean pull and push methods. We shore up existing infrastructure to withstand future DYS infiltration.

For yourself and those you live with and work with, give the brain a boost, take a breath, de-stress.

When we unburden our brains from unproductive, stressful busyness, we zero in on what matters. We change the feed. We zap DYS to cleanse our work atmosphere and to reverse unhealthy trends. With active mindfulness, we maintain awareness of harmful social, physical, and virtual content. By sharing mindfulness based strategies we improve the day to day and the long term.

With a healthful breath, discover your full brain potential. Write a poem. How about an acrostic poem? Use the word:

D

I

S

C

O

V

E

R

Share your poems. What other words inspire you?

Walk, run, exercise, practice yoga, in the moment.

With each walk, each run, each exercise on an elliptical machine, each yoga pose, meditate on movement, on rhythm, on sound, and on the "I am." This is your "I am" in the moment, aware, mind de-cluttered, daily re-connection. Reap the rewards of building grey matter.

Practicing mindfulness builds leadership skills associated with EQ, SQ, and CQ. This book emphasizes the crucial role of emotional and cultural intelligence in creating and sustaining *OH&F*, healthy human relationships, and strong and fit working environments.

Analyze and resolve, write your story.

You have practiced mindfulness, re-discovered creativity, and centered yourself. Analyze the situation and move forward with solutions. Define a situation that needs attention. For example, inadequate communication or toxic behavior due to unexpected changes. Decide on one objective. With situation and objective in mind formulate potential solutions. Write a narrative as though you were writing a short story.

Write your narrative.

Explore five ending possibilities.

- For each, map it, write it, draw it, sing it, play it, reshape it, collaborate.
- Remember lean principles of communication with each player in the solutions chain; before and after you.

Examine the five possibilities and decide on which would be the

- best of all worlds,
- the most realistic,
- the most likely to succeed.

Individually and/or in teams write five versions of the same story.

1. The happy ending with the solutions implemented successfully thereby achieving the objective.
2. Unhappy ending with the solutions not implemented successfully and therefore the objective not achieved.
3. As in classic drama in life, solutions implemented and objective achieved with something precious lost.
4. Sacrificing the implementation of all solutions and the realization of the objective for a greater good.
5. An ambiguous or bittersweet ending.

Return to the five endings of each story.

In all cases how do they mirror your real life situations?

1. The happy ending with the solutions successfully implemented and the objective achieved – keep in mind the conditions necessary for implementing the solutions to achieve this objective. How long lasting will the solutions be? How realistic and doable is this narrative?

2. Unhappy ending with the solutions implemented unsuccessfully and objective not achieved – what prevents the solutions from being implemented? Is it an unrealistic timeline, ineffective communication, inadequate buy in? Why  is the objective unrealistic? Is the situation beyond repair? What causes underlie this scenario?

3. As in classic drama, objective achieved with something else lost – what has been lost? What in your solutions implementation has caused the loss? How has your sense of accomplishment been diminished by this loss?

4. Sacrificing the objective for a greater good – what characteristics of the objective make it unachievable? Describe the greater good and how you measure the greater good. How lasting will it be? How does sacrificing the objective make the greater good worthwhile?

5. An ambiguous or bittersweet ending – what caused the ambiguity? Which goals have been achieved and which ones  haven't? Does the "sweetness" outweigh all else? Is the glass still half full for you as an optimist? You have crossed the finish line in this marathon though not in first place. How much does first place matter?

3   CORE TEAM APPROACH TO ZAPPING DYS

With honest, mindful appraisals we recognize when complacency and cynicism creep in to fill lapses with behaviors that threaten organizational muscle. We combat toxic behaviors to maintain muscle for resilience in changing times.

CORE teams implement real solutions by filling voids or gaps with common sense recipes. Through the CORE team approach we share knowledge from past experience. We distinguish between temporary, pumped up on steroids versus lean, sustainable muscle. We differentiate necessary from unnecessary growth. With a lean philosophy we choose sustainable operations mindful of precious human energy.

Head in the Sand? Causes and Symptoms? What to Do?

Ignorance is not bliss! Head in the sand can result in dangerous brain malfunction leading to an ailing circulatory system. This cuts essential oxygen supply. What do we do about oxygen deprivation? We create mindfulness practice opportunities. We attack symptoms by foregoing the blame game choosing instead a sincere search for long term solutions. We facilitate mindful problem solving strategies.

We restore circulatory health with honest appraisals to implement realistic plans. We avoid dictatorial leadership. We use EQ and CQ to match adaptive engaged full brain leadership strategies to situations.

CORE Team Observations and Advice

Without change preparedness, communication lapses and gaps in leadership provide DYS the opportunity to slip into your infrastructure.

Opportunistic DYS attacks the weakest links. In times of change avoid giving DYS an inroad. Do not allow it to infiltrate your good common sense and established building blocks. Shore up your gaps with solid communication. Bind your lapses with indisputable ethics. Provide the mindfulness rich environment necessary for *OH&F* that reflects your collective essence. Champion trust as your cornerstone promoting individual integrity and ethics at all levels.

Growth, mergers, acquisitions, shifting company focus responding to market and economic trends represent predictable and unpredictable changes. Full implementation of changes takes time. Mindfully manage change preparedness, readiness, and response.

Be mindful that growth without a healthy infrastructure and change preparedness invites DYS. Growth for the sake of growth may not have the intended results. There is much to say for a lean approach to an entity's management and evolution in all sectors.

Without a preparedness plan even predictable change can have unpredictable ramifications. Unpredictability can create havoc without change readiness. Bringing awareness to a solid foundation goes a long way toward mitigating negative reactions to unforeseen changes. Honest, meaningful communication at all levels of a non-threatening listen and learn environment results in effective change response. Mindfully involve brain and heart.

Facilitate the path to real and lasting solutions through adaptive leadership. Understand and maintain sensitivity to each situation and to your diverse and collective cultures. No matter how sophisticated your human resources (HR) database, your talent capital represents much more than numbers, date hired, date left. Go beyond HR tallies of benefits, reviews, and promotions. Involve your HR staff in decisions on HR policy. With involvement your HR staff will whole heartedly supports *OH&F* with hiring and review practices that focus on talent development and retention. In a healthy environment, HR staff bolsters *OH&F* through positive interactions with potential, new, and existing employees. It promotes horizontal learning. HR reflects the mindful philosophy to, "develop employees so well that they can leave and treat them so well that they want to stay."

Be innovative. We all have had mentors, people that made a difference in our lives. Put on their hats. What would she or he do? Bring daily awareness to your actions. Use the full powers of your EQ and CQ. Provide the physical and mental space for mindfulness.

Identify existing individual and group strengths. Build on them. Strength comes from people. We can never say this enough. Build individual talent for success. Replace indecisiveness with clarity. Replace lip service. with substantive communication.

Build your integrity muscle. Champion personal integrity at all levels. This message should be communicated without dilution. Well-articulated ethics build resilience and loyalty.

Don't allow DYS to undermine your infrastructure. Make it clear that everyone's efforts matter. Convey without reservations, your appreciation of the professional, social, and personal cultures of all individuals that make up your fabric. Use communication approaches and language appropriate to your cultures.

Regularly conduct *OH&F* checkups. Use the tools that make the most sense for your current health profile and for your future *OH&F* goals. With creativity, design your own tools for gauging your combined people power.

After examining your *OH&F* checkup results reaffirm your strengths and implement plans to shore up any shortcomings. Stay true to the course of maintaining *OH&F* on and off site, physical and virtual. A healthy workplace equals happy, engaged employees. *OH&F* increases employee retention and the triple bottom line.

Your plan of action to maintain *OH&F* recognizes the value of your human talent treasure. Attuned to sustainable, lean management, you do not squander human talent, your most valued resource. The happy, satisfied, employee feeds the profit bottom line that you display to your investor or constituents. As McKinsey reports reaffirm, organizational health is a competitive advantage.

People oriented, mindful businesses and institutions, run their operations by valuing human stamina and a healthy physical and virtual working environment. Poor *OH&F* undermines stamina which wastes energy. Squandered human energy leads to poor physical and emotional vitals. Furthermore, wasted human energy undermines productivity. Adopt lean management techniques that emphasize waste minimization. Conserving human energy for positive tasks develops individual talents. This contributes to fulfilling larger, long-lasting *OH&F* goals.

Be bold; take your employees' pulse. Ask and they will share what would make them fully engaged for your collective success. Employees delineate your path to *OH&F*. Remember the proven best practice for success pays close attention to the triple bottom line, people, planet, and profit.

Take vitals. Follow the survey suggestions or formulate your own. Do this regularly to stay on top of any DYS incursions. Important topics: employee retention, employee engagement.

Take the break for lunch suggested on the next page. Discover and celebrate your strengths.

Lunch Break
Discover Your Strengths Exercise
Power Plates

Time needed for this in person team exercise: approximately two hours -- A half an hour for instructions and preparation and one hour and a half for enjoying pot luck, multi-cultural buffet lunch.

When: Over a pot luck buffet lunch with courses made by participants – salads and main course items served separately from desserts. Facilitators can choose theme, preferably with input incorporating your diverse and combined cultures. Themes can include celebrating company anniversary, a new contract, holidays, and always the culinary delights inspired by multi-cultural diversity.

Materials: white paper plates and multi-colored markers.

- Before the pot luck buffet lunch – announce the power plates. Distribute five plates per person and colored markers.
- Ask participants to use the plates to note five strengths about themselves, personal or at work. "I am good at…" These can be one or several per plate and on additional plates as needed.
- Facilitate exchange and sharing of the power plates responses.
- Once lunch is set up ask participants to walk toward buffet lunch placing the plates to line their paths.
- Ask all to walk back to their seats switching paths to have a chance to read others' positives as they approach their tables.
- Repeat exercise during dessert. Ask participants to write positives about colleagues varying the path back to tables.
- Make this a longer lunch, take your time, enjoy, and have fun.

Encourage poems, stories, illustrations. Top your competition with a literary and arts blog open to all!

Decorate your workplace with your power plates. Sky's the limit!

Assess Your Working Environment's *OH&F* Vitals

Encourage your CORE team to do this with focus groups, interviews, and surveys. Here are some topics and questions for you to consider:

Tip: use open-ended questions, get permissions, record responses. Ask questions pertinent to sustainable *OH&F*:

- Define an ideal size for your group, company, or agency.
- How would it improve if it were larger?
- How would it improve if it were smaller?
- On a 1-4 scale with 4 as best, how well can you and your organization sustain change in market focus, in location, in staff, in service or specialty realignment, in technology?
- Describe the strengths in specialty areas? How is your company, agency, or nonprofit poised for the future?
- How does your employee retention stack up? How about your employee engagement?
- Describe current measures to retain human capital. What approaches do you suggest for happy, engaged employees who thrive and give back through their creativity and growth?
- How do you interpret the triple bottom line -- of people, planet, and profit? How does your organization define it?

You've done your analysis. Now enjoy a creative break.

Draw what happiness means to you.
Create your own clip art.

A poem, a song, a dance.
A happy employee…
A happy boss…
Happy to me… to you… to us… means…

Draw your individual and group versions of the triple bottom line, people – planet – profit and your keystone.

A couple of versions below depict the triple bottom line and a variation on that formula with trust as the keystone. What interpretations of the triple bottom line formula do you have?

What are your individual and group thoughts on the importance of trust to your interpretations of the triple bottom line?

In a group exercise, incorporate how social and work environments make an impact on the bottom line.

How would you measure the "value" of human capital – people – and natural capital – planet – within the context of profit, resilience. Carry those measures to other triple bottom line interpretations.

Adjust the visual depictions to your liking, free form, diagrams, charts, whatever flows for you and… communicates your views.

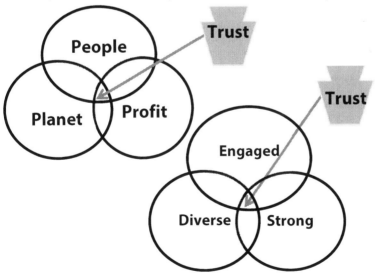

 Mindfulness – Re-Minder

Trust and nurture your CORE teams. You can count on them.

Discussion Points for Solutions
Implementing *OH&F*

Examine paths to improving *OH&F*, the what, why, how, who:
- What evident gaps/voids surface?
- Why do gaps/voids exist?
- How does imbalance manifest itself?
- What symptoms appear and which prevail?
- How to best re-calibrate and transform?

Implementation strategies:
- Build on strengths.
- Lay out realistic, phased paths to lasting *OH&F*.
- Use optimum social and cultural intelligence to collaborate.
- Share responsibilities.

Tools and solutions:
- Interview current and past employees to identify strengths.
- Take charge of each phase of the implementation timeline.
- CORE team enlists interior and exterior mentors to resolve challenges.
- Track and communicate changes in vitals and environment.

Customize or use suggested 7 qualities of a successful leader:
1. Exemplary character – personal integrity.
2. Enthusiastic, sincere communicator.
3. Confident in delegating and succession planning.
4. Focused on vision, purpose, empathy, and ethics.
5. Mindful, calm, sensitive to professional and personal cultures.
6. Engaged full brain, analytical, problem solver, creative thinker.
7. Dedicated to a culture of loyalty built on trust.

4 DYS ZAPPED, WORKPLACE TRANSFORMED – FOUR PHASES

We undertake each DYS eradication and working environment transformation operation with a four-phased approach. The next chapter details the metaphorical tools we use for each of our four phases of investigation, cleanup, eradication, and prevention.

During Phase 1 we gather preliminary data through research, onsite interviews, observation, and preliminary measurements. In Phase 2 we follow a strict environmental contamination sampling protocol for DYS sampling. In Phase 3 we conduct customized contamination cleansing and remediation. The post-remediation, Phase 4, integrates data with lessons learned to achieve lasting *OH&F*.

Four Phases

Phase 1 – Collect and interpret onsite and offsite data to gauge the potential for DYS virus contamination.

Phase 2 – Gather onsite samples with specialized tools to determine the presence of the DYS virus.

Phase 3 – Carry out focused cleaning and disinfection with tools appropriate for the tasks at hand.

Phase 4 – Formulate the action plan for implementing solutions to eradicate current and potential DYS attacks.

Data clouds for tracking DYS reoccurrence

We encourage accuracy and consistency in data and document management. In our system, we gather and consult data on our secure clouds specific to each type of investigation. For fun, we give our data cloud metaphoric names that relate to our ecosphere.

- **Cumulus** – For **first time or ongoing** investigations we populate and consult our low, accessible, cumulus data cloud.
- **Altostratus** – For **DYS dormant for at least five years**, we pull data from the middle level, altostratus data cloud.
- **Cirrus** – For **archived incidents that occurred more than 10 years ago** and **have not reappeared**. We visit the high layers of cirrus cloud data, for lessons learned from sustained *OH&F*.

The How – Identification, Cure, and Prevention

Using our tools and methodology we assess whether viral attacks to our pillars of strength, resilience, integrity, and their accompanying essential structural elements have driven down resistance to DYS.

Phase 1 – Research and onsite observations

We combine historical information received from DYSpatch and stored in our databases with our onsite reconnaissance observations. Our Mindfulness Owl Eyes tools search for any potential for DYS viral contamination. We capture images of the areas for return visits as needed. During this phase we plan our sampling protocol.

We upload our visual data gathered through our Mindfulness Owl Eyes mobile app into a database that matches historical with current images and notes. This sets the scene for DYS treatment solutions.

The preliminary sampling protocol calls for sweeping behind cabinets and corners with our DYStrapper treated dust mop. Once we gather evidence visible to the naked eye, our DYScatcher analyzes these airborne particles matching findings with visual data.

Warning signs of presence or resurgence of DYS can manifest themselves as follows. Behind and under desks, wedged in drawers; printouts of emails from upper and middle management, in large bold letters, many in red, addressed to staff, dismissing telework options. Fast food containers stacked in a majority of employees' trash cans point to employees working late, leaving hurriedly. Few, if any, personal items in cubicles to personalize work spaces, unprofessional email protocol, unhealthful snacking, impersonal atmosphere, closed mindedness about telework, all produce toxic consequences.

Phase 2 – Physical sampling

We move into Phase 2, sampling of particles too minute for the naked eye. If data and interviews tell us that turnover of employees in the preceding couple of years has been substantial, we must ascertain the magnitude of the DYS virus. For extensive physical sampling we dig deep with magnifying equipment augmenting Phase 1 evidence.

Phase 3 – Remediation – cleanup

Whether we tackle a new case or a recurrence, the CORE team plans a thorough cleansing and disinfection with the essential assistance of colleagues and mentors. We continue to ask questions, listen and learn as we implement our cleanup.

Our cleanup procedures match each situation. We may decide to clean out the DYS contaminants with the industrial strength DYSxtrator. Our strategy remains constant; we involve the CORE team at every step. Its members know which infrastructure elements need urgent attention and in what order. They concentrate on specific touch points. For cleansing beyond the superficial, there must be a buy-in at all levels.

Phase 4 – Action plan for implementing lasting solutions

When analysis identifies mistrust of upper management expressed by staff, the antidote: good dose of empathy, kindness, fairness, and respect, consistently reinforced and communicated. To break the DYS cause and effect cycle we suggest realistic goals. What we facilitate must be an effective, easy pill to swallow. Our approaches include negotiation a give and take, with clear goals as to outcome.

The solution phase includes:

- Interviewing, surveying individuals at all levels.
- Creating "safe" communication havens.
- Recognizing and developing individual talent with cross-training and consistently fair behavior.
- Giving useful employee reviews aimed at career growth.

And a gym membership for all!

Example of Cause and Effect

Cause - Void
Leadership Change or Inconsistency

Effect
Confusion

Symptom
Stress

Effect
Leave Job

 Mindfulness – Re-Minder

Listen and learn. Mentor others.
Document problem solving strategies for future challenges.

5 DYS ZAPPED, WORK ENVIRONMENT TRANSFORMED – TOOLS

In this chapter our metaphorical tools emphasize the importance of accurately documenting, classifying, and integrating DYS evidence. We encourage you to customize your tools. Document your successes and failures to better understand how to regain and maintain your *OH&F*. Have fun with our data cloud and tool names and functions!

Adapting Tools to Your Data Clouds to Manage Data Well

We advise to match tools to data upload and retrieval. Our DYSpatch ER Center provides us with background information and statistics for each DYS incident. Well-equipped in the latest tracking, zapping, and transformation technology, it mines its databases matching them to natural cloud storage properties. Store and consult data appropriate to your *OH&F* needs.

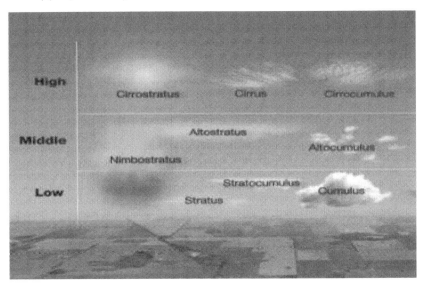

In the high cirrus cloud we learn from transformed workplaces where DYS has been eradicated for over ten years.

Where DYS has been identified and eradicated more than once within the last five years, we tap the mid-level, altostratus cloud. These data assist in uncovering clues about reoccurrence and DYS's resistance to remedies. Here we learn about particularly virulent cases.

For first time occurrences or recently recurrent DYS we store, share, and consult the low, easily accessible cumulus cloud data. During our work week journey, we use cloud data appropriate to our five workplaces and five VIPs.

Each DYSpatch notification comes with the appropriate cloud database information transferred securely to cell phones or tablets. The seriousness of the condition activates communication tools necessary for our experts conducting offsite and onsite investigations. We establish baselines, and then identify deviations from the norm. With robust redundancy methods, our tools populate databases.

Our missions and time limitations always take continuity of operations into account. This means we must knowledgeably use DYS virus zapping tools. Our advancements in customized apps for smart devices continue to make the job of identifying and remediating DYS easier for our CORE team. Technology gives the CORE team a leg up with apps specific to measuring *OH&F* and tracking evidence of DYS.

Sampling and Remediation Tools

At the initial observation stage we use the DYScover stethoscope to measure *OH&F* pulse and heartbeat for sluggishness, stress, or wasted energy. We listen for regularity of heartbeat and pulse.

The DYStrapper coating on cleaning supplies allows the collection of DYS virus particles down to molecular levels quick and accurate. Quickness and accuracy in identifying DYS lead to timely resolutions promoting faster recovery. Of note are the Mindfulness Owl Eyes 360° Camera and three ways MagnifEye apps includes Microscope mobile apps, developed specifically for this purpose.

We integrate data from onsite and offsite workspaces. We observe and sample, offices, cubicles, common meeting and eating areas. If accessible and appropriate we gather data from offsite client locations. The growth of telecommuting dictates that we research work environments in homes and other teleworking situations.

DYSweeper Broom - sweeps out hidden DYS particles from under rugs and anti-static mats.

DYScard Dust Pan – anti DYS coated captures, eliminates, and discards remnants of DYS.

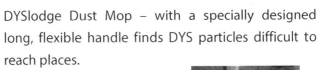

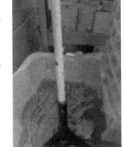

DYSlodge Dust Mop – with a specially designed long, flexible handle finds DYS particles difficult to reach places.

DYStructor Wet Mop - washes out surfaces coated with DYS, with an anti-DYS solution.

DYSvacuator Cleaners - capture DYS invisible particles remaining after sweeping and mopping.

DYSxtractor Industrial Strength Extractor – eradicates removes

persistent DYS infections.

Mindful Owl Eyes mobile apps

The Owl Three-Way MagnifEye app serves as a:

1. Magnifying glass for tiny, hidden DYS particles.

2. Microscope for cellular particles to test the toxicity of new or re-occurring DYS presence.

3. Muscle indicator, to determine DYS presence as it relates to inability to withstand challenges due to decreased muscle strength.

Mindful Owl ObservEye 360° Camera Macro to Zoom App for investigating the work environment, mapping geography and landscape. With infrared capability operated from a drone, it audits environment's positive energy retention and permeability balance. This capability gauges OH&F's level of permeability that allows for the extraction of negative DYS elements and the entry of essential nourishment.

Mindful Owl ReflectEye Mirror App regular and enlarging for looking inside and outside a face. It reflects individual and collective image and self-image. It checks perception versus reality for individuals and groups.

We encourage you to document your solutions implementation path at every turn to gauge success and setbacks. Use specialized data storage, onsite, offsite. Customize your own cloud banks. Communicate access to information at every level.

List your short term and long term objectives for sustained *OH&F*.

- Your goal is sustained *OH&F*.
- Fill in a timeline with realistic objectives toward that goal.
- Be generous with the timeline for well thought out phasing toward sustained *OH&F*.
- For best results, do it right, not fast.
- There are successes. Celebrate these
- There are failures. There are mistakes.
    - Recognize these as they occur.
    - Learn from them.
    - Don't let them linger and develop into bigger issues.
    - Deal with them promptly.
- Document your lessons learned. Celebrate them.

Give visibility to your objectives by drawing them.

- Make them real.
- Have fun.
- Want to make your plan to work, use humor. Nothing like humor to bring the message home.

Using engaged full brain, mindful, analytical, and creative methods, discuss, plan, draw, and work through your group solutions for zapping DYS and transforming your work environment.

Outline or map your dynamic plan and your realistic goals. Make it doable, make it real, and make it work for everyone.

- A. Short term – 6 months to one year
- B. One to two years
- C. Long term – two to five years
- D. Sustained *OH&F*

What are your tools for your short term plan?

- Create them.
- Adjust them.
- Document them.
- Share them.

How could your tools change with each of your phased plans?

Let your EQ, CQ, and SQ guide you.

Be bold.

Be focused.

Be mindful.

Be kind.

Sing a song that reminds you of someone or something.

6 TAKE A CREATIVE BREAK – ENGAGE YOUR FULL BRAIN THINKING – BRAINSTORMING – GAMESTORMING

At least once a day, treat yourself to a few minutes to take a deep breath break. Travel with awareness of your breath slowly. Try to alternate between belly and diaphragm; five breaths each.

Fill your lungs with breath, five times, slowly. Bring awareness to your diaphragm; fill it with breath five times. Deep, five belly full breaths. Breathe in, slowly, breathe out slowly, and become aware of the space between breaths. Relax your shoulders. Enjoy the feeling. Travel with your breath relaxing shoulders, neck, behind your eyes, eyes, nose, ears, cranium, and forehead.

If you find yourself tense, reacting with anger, get out of your fight / flight triggered mode with a few quick breaths through your nose. Give permission to that oxygen infusion to calm you.

The Magic of Breathing

Owls take breaks too.

Pick a pose. Pick a picture.
Draw your own.

Take a yoga break.

How would you communicate calm?

- Draw calm? How about quiet, draw quiet.
- Write calm, write quiet.
- Reflect on: "Wisdom needs my attention."
- Share your thoughts on lean management principles.

33

Meditate and Create

Meditate on the now, give your brain a rest, build your grey matter.

Picasso said: "If you want to paint close your eyes and sing a song."

This is your space. Your calm place. Give it a try.

Write a few words, a surprise, a poem, or think it , let it flow down a calm stream nestled in mountains, sit on clouds you've noticed recently, travel with a great blue heron, hum it, find your calm place.

Try a golden shovel poem! Take a poem or a saying you like or someone else likes. Choose one line, take each word of that line and use each word as an end line to your poem. No rhyming needed, punctuation up to you. Make it a team effort.

 Mindfulness – Re-Minder

With mindfulness we practice how to differentiate between information and wisdom. Our tools give us information, information gives us knowledge. With experience we transform knowledge into wisdom, wisdom into effective action.

TAKE A CREATIVE BREAK – ENGAGE YOUR FULL BRAIN THINKING –
BRAINSTORMING – GAMESTORMING

Group or Individual Exercises

Connect these dots with four lines without lifting your pencil –
and… resist using Google for the answer.

Take your time, throw away frustration, allow the trying and re-
trying to bring you calm. Draw nine dots on separate sheets of paper;
allow the meditative trial and error process to carry you. Try it again.

Enjoy the calm that concentration provides. Try and re-try. Resist
Googling for the answer.

Explore lines, draw concentric circles, spirals. What do closed
circles versus spirals represent for you, for your co-workers?

routines

new things

**Do it and talk about it. What are the pluses, the minuses? How do
these illustrate your transformation plans?**

This is your space to take a pause, reflect, with engaged full brain thinking, brainstorm, gamestorm, have fun!

For ideas check out www.gamestorming.com/. Use diagrams, draw cartoons alone and collectively. One draw a face, another add, eyes, arms. Draw animals, buildings, abstracts, clouds, waves, geometric shapes, have fun.

What animals come to mind when you think "mindful." Don't overthink it, be spontaneous. Be in the moment, enjoy it.

What crucial elements does the group want to include to demonstrate achieving *OH&F*? Triangles, circles, lines, arrows, try it.

On an index card everyone Write down feelings experienced with mindfulness practice. Shuffle the cards. Take Turns reading the cards.

What other key Word could fill the triangles?

Inside triangle labels: OH&F Achieved · Mindfulness · Org Leadership · Org Strength

How would this triangle look reversed? What words would be the same, different?

Engaged Full Brain Thinking – Brainstorm 1: Brainstorm about animals that have the index card characteristics. On butcher block paper create a portable mural with several animals. As a group, decide on the audience that will view your mural. Formulate your message.

Note Ned Hermann's model. Put the animal(s) in a situation with other animals and/or human engaging the characteristics of the four areas of engaged full brain thinking.

Facts

Form

Feelings

Future

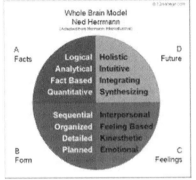

Which quadrants do you tend to call on the most? Take a survey of your colleagues. Do you discern a reliance on certain cognitive areas of your individual full brain capacity, your competencies? How is your collective, engaged, full brain thinking?

Engaged Full Brain Thinking – Brainstorm 2: Individually take time to write your approaches to the same scenario. Scenario: your company will merge with an international conglomerate. Define your current collective culture. Take turns reading each version of someone else's narrative. Document the similarities. Document the differences. Convince the M&A partners that retaining your existing collective culture is essential for success in the restructure.

Come together as a group; create a combined narrative agreeable to all. Discuss lessons learned in this collaborative effort.

Decide on your audience(s). Provide illustrations for the culture preservation rationale. Publish your illustrated narrative internally or launch it to the world. Exhibit your illustrations.

Ask colleagues not involved in this exercise to write poems, stories, or songs to your drawings.

With analysis, experience, creativity we build DYS prevention.

When we build *OH&F* we prevent DYS from entering
Our work and life space.
When we prevent DYS
We prevent its domino effect.
When we build *OH&F*
We make this a better world to work and live in.

 **Take a deep breath break, five minutes at least.
Trust creativity.**

Now, you're ready to consider individual and working environment vital signs.

> ### Mindfulness – Re-Minder
>
> When we are self-aware and self-confident, we invite kindness and compassion into our actions. With kindness and compassion we build *OH&F*. With strong *OH&F we* all benefit.

7 INDIVIDUAL AND WORKING ENVIRONMENT VITAL SIGNS

In this chapter we demonstrate measuring tools for gauging individual as well as environmental vital signs. Using the public health promotion paradigm in this book we suggest interviewing individual employees to gauge their emotional and physical well-being. We measure the characteristics of the working environment as viewed by employees at several professional levels. Thus, we capture realities and perceptions.

These measuring tools are meant to be adapted. Included are results for two *OH&F* perspectives in a medium sized engineering firm;

1. one by an administrative staff person and the
2. second by a project manager.

They are surveyed for two types of health profiles;

A. their emotional and physical state, and their
B. view of others versus their self-view.

We provide blank fillable forms for additional surveys. Take this opportunity for discussion, honest evaluations of potential DYS infiltration, and planning for long-term DYS prevention.

We measure individual vital signs of emotional, physical, and balanced well-being by interviewing individual employees. They report their heart, pulse, energy, and stress levels to give results to be tallied and discussed.

With these tools we mindfully assess the impact of the working environment on individual employees. The more we know, the more we can put the results and observations toward the ultimate goal of preventing DYS and achieving sustained *OH&F*.

Sample Results of Individual
Vital Signs – Perspective 1

Mid-Sized Engineering Company – *1 to 4 (4 as best), Vital Signs 12 = 100% – Emotional and Physical State 16 = 100%*

Title/Role(s): **Administrative Staff, Front Office**

Responsibilities: Administrative staff who handles day to day, scheduling, calls, assists with accounting, request for proposals (RFPs) production, and marketing.

Vital Signs: Heart 4/12 = 33% – Pulse 3/12 = 25% – Energy 4/12 = 33% – Stress 3/12 = 25%

Emotional and Physical State:

Emotional 4/16 = 25% – Physical 5/16 = 31% – Work Life Balance 5/16 = 31%

Vital Signs	Heart	4	Pulse	3	Energy	4	Stress	3	
Emotional	Calm	1	Content	1	Creative	1	Confident	1	4
Physical	Stable	2	Strong	1	Steady	1	Relaxed	1	5
Balance (W L)	Happy	1	Constant	1	Fulfilled	2	Low Stress	1	5

Recap of results by CORE team.

Sample Results of Working Environment Vital Signs – Perspective 1

Mid-Sized Engineering Company – *1 to 4 (4 as best)*,
Environment 20 = 100% – View of Others and Self-View 16 = 100%

Title/Role(s): **Administrative Staff, Front Office**

Responsibilities: Administrative support staff who handles day to day, scheduling, calls, assists with accounting, RFP production, and marketing.

Environment: Conduct: 10/20 = 50% – Message 10/20 = 50% – Leadership 9/20 = 45% – Engagement 8/20 = 40%

View of Others: UM 7/16 = 44% – MM 7/16 = 44% – PM 9/16 = 63% – PS 8/16 = 50% – CW 8/16 = 50%

Self -View: See highlighted row. *Loyal Hoping Org Conduct Will Change 3 – Informed by Org Message 2 – Responsive to Leadership Hoping Non Dictatorial Leadership Will Change Course 3 – Positive on Current Engagement Policies 2 – Total 10/16 = 63%*

Environ-ment	Org Conduct	10	Org Message	10	Leader-ship	9	Engage-ment	8	
Upper Mgmt.	Respect-ful	2	Mindful	2	Ethical	2	Clear Policy	1	7
Middle Mgmt.	Impartial	2	Consistent	1	Proactive	2	Affirming	2	7
Project Mgrs.	Objective	2	Sincere	3	Support WL Balance	2	Apprecia-tive	2	9
Prof Staff	Trust-worthy	3	Focused	3	Optimistic	1	Enthusias-tic	1	8
Admin Staff	*Loyal*	*3*	*Informed*	*2*	*Responsive*	*3*	*Positive*	*2*	*10*
Clients' Views	Upbeat	2	Clear	2	Accessible	2	Commit-ted	2	8

How does this employee's role influence responses?

Sample Results of Individual
Vital Signs – Perspective 2

Mid-Sized Engineering Company – *1 to 4 (4 as best), Vital Signs 12 = 100% – Emotional and Physical State 16 = 100%*

Title/Role(s):   **Project Manager, Public Sector Projects**

Responsibilities: Project manager who reports to a middle management, section manager. Handles majority of public sector projects, on site.

Vital Signs: Heart 4/12= 33% – Pulse 3/12 = 25% – Energy 4/12 = 33% – Reflexes 3/12 = 33%

Emotional and Physical State:
Emotional 4/16 = 25% – Physical 5/16 = 31% – Work Life Balance 5/16 = 31%

Vitals	Heart	4	Pulse	3	Senses	4	Reflexes	3	
Emotional	Calm	1	Content	1	Creative	1	Confident	1	4
Physical	Stable	2	Steady	1	Stamina	1	Relaxed	1	5
W L Balance	Happy	1	Constant	1	Valued	2	Low Stress	1	5

Recap of results by CORE team:

**Sample Results of Working Environment
Vital Signs– Perspective 2**

Mid-Sized Engineering Company – *1 to 4 (4 as best),
Environment 20 = 100% – View of Others and Self-View 16 = 100%*

Title/Role(s):   **Project Manager, Public Sector Projects**

Responsibilities: Project manager who reports to a middle management section manager. Handles majority of public sector projects on site.

Environment: Conduct: 11/20 = 55% – Message 14/20 = 58% – Leadership 12/20 = 50% – Engagement 11/20 = 46%

View of Others: UM 7/16 = 44% - MM 6/16 = 38% - PM 9/16 = 63% - PS 7/16 = 44% – CW 8/16 = 50%

Self -View: See highlighted row. *Objective Hoping Org Conduct Will Change 3 , Own Org Message Sincere 4, Supportive of Work Live Balance 3, Appreciates Engagement Hoping that Non Dictatorial Leadership Will have Clear Policy 3– Total 13/16 = 81%*

Environ-ment	Org Conduct	11	Org Message	12	Leader-ship	10	Engage-ment	11	
Upper Mgmt.	Respect-ful	3	Mindful	3	Ethical	3	Clear Policy	1	**10**
Middle Mgmt.	Impartial	1	Consistent	1	Proactive	2	Affirming	2	**6**
Project Mgrs.	*Objective*	*3*	*Sincere*	*4*	*Support WL Balance*	*3*	*Apprecia-tive*	*3*	*13*
Prof Staff	Trust-worthy	3	Focused	3	Optimistic	1	Enthusi-astic	1	**8**
Admin Staff	Loyal	2	Informed	2	Responsive	3	Positive	2	**9**
Clients' View	Upbeat	2	Clear	3	Accessible	2	Commit-ted	2	**9**

How does this employee's role influence responses?

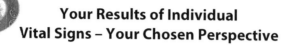

Your Results of Individual
Vital Signs – Your Chosen Perspective

Organization _____ – *1 to 4 (4 as best),*
Vital Signs 12 = 100% – Emotional and Physical State 16 = 100%

Title/Role(s):   _____

Responsibilities: _____

                       _____

Vital Signs: Heart _____ = __% – Pulse _____= __% – Energy
                       _____ = __% – Reflexes _____ = __%

Emotional and Physical State:
                       Emotional _____ = __% – Physical _____ = __% –
                       Work Life Balance _____ = __%

My Vitals	Heart		Pulse		Senses		Reflexes		Add
Emotional	Calm		Content		Creative		Confident		
Physical	Stable		Steady		Stamina		Relaxed		
W L Balance	Happy		Constant		Valued		Low Stress		
Totals									

Recap of results by your CORE team:

**As a group collaboration exercise you can redesign this measuring
tool and use categories to fit your situation.**

Your Results of Working Environment Vital Signs – Your Chosen Perspective

Organization_____ – *1 to 4 (4 as best),*
Environment 20 = 100% – View of Others and Self-View 16 = 100%

Title/Role(s): _____

Responsibilities: _____
_____

Environment: Conduct: _____ = __% – Message _____ = __% –
Leadership _____ = __% – Engagement _____ =
__%

View of Others: 5 of 6 – __ _____ = __% – __ _____ = __% – __
_____ = __% – __ _____ = __% – __ _____ = __%

Self -View: *Observation_____ __,*
Observation _____ __,
Observation _____ __,
Observation _____ ___ – Total ____ = __%

Environ-ment	Org Conduct	Message	Leadership	Engagement	Add
Upper Mgmt.	Respectful	Mindful	Ethical	Clear Policy	
Middle Mgmt.	Impartial	Consistent	Proactive	Appreciative	
Project Mgrs.	Objective	Sincere	Have W L Balance	Affirming	
Prof Staff	Trusting	Focused	Optimistic	Enthusiastic	
Admin Staff	Loyal	Informed	Responsive	Positive	
Clients' View	Upbeat	Clear	Accessible	Committed	
Totals					

How does this employee's role influence responses?

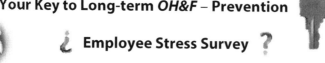

Your Key to Long-term *OH&F* – Prevention

¿ Employee Stress Survey ?

Why – Example: there has been a downward trend in the level of employee engagement, increase in employee flight, both leading to palpable low morale. There are symptoms of dictatorial leadership.

What – Assumption: stress at work causes a reduction in employee engagement ultimately leading to employee flight. Having a culture that allows for alleviating stress by dealing with stressful situations through sincere, open discussions, internally.

How – Four questions:
1. Do you feel stressed more than once a week?
2. Can you discuss stress with your immediate manager or supervisor?
3. Would you rather discuss stress with your co-workers?
4. Would you rather discuss stress with your family and friends?

Mid-Sized Consulting Firm
Survey Results – 65 Employees

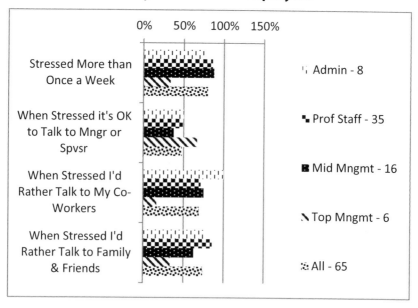

Your Key to Long-term *OH&F* – DYS Prevention

 ¿ **Reduce Stress – Employee Stress Survey** ?

Take time and break down the questions to fit your situation.

Why – Describe the reason for conducting a stress survey; symptoms, behaviors, effect on engagement, etc.

- Document individual and collective thoughts on the "why."

What – Discuss what causes stress in the working environment.

- Do certain conditions dominate?

How – Gauge how often the person feels stressed and the effect of stress on their physical and mental well-being.

- Does the person feel stressed more than once a week?
- How do frequency, patterns, and responses to unpredictable situations cause or alleviate stress?

Who – Stress in the workplace is best handled within the environment where it occurs as opposed to bringing stress home. Ideally, stress should be discussed as easily with management as with colleagues.

- Can the person discuss his or her stressful situations with the immediate manager or supervisor?
- Within the given culture, can the management accept experimentation and failure as signs of growth and creativity? Remember the motto in all good science, "failure is not an option, it is a requirement." Failures are our best lessons in life.
- Would the employee rather discuss stress with co-workers than with management or immediate boss?
- Assess the internal culture in terms of expression, open discussions without defensiveness and feelings of failure.
- Would the employee rather discuss stress with family and friends that with co-workers or immediate boss? Why?

Tally What Your Organization Does Well

Circle 1 (does not do) – 2 (does somewhat, can improve) – 3 (pretty good can improve slightly) – 4 (doing well)

Image presented by your organization to your clients

- Trust   1   2   3   4
- Integrity   1   2   3   4
- Consistency in message to the public   1   2   3   4
- Community involvement   1   2   3   4
- Diversity in staff   1   2   3   4
- Knowing staff, being known by name   1   2   3   4

Does Well = 24

Your individual view about your company/organization

- Trust   1   2   3   4
- Integrity   1   2   3   4
- Consistency in message to the public   1   2   3   4
- Community involvement   1   2   3   4
- Diversity in staff   1   2   3   4
- Knowing staff, being known by name   1   2   3   4

Does Well = 24

Tally What Your Organization Does Well

Circle 1 (does not do) – 2 (does somewhat, can improve) – 3 (pretty good can improve slightly) – 4 (doing well)

Promote and nurture a healthy work environment

• Trust between colleagues	1 2 3 4
• Fairness in promotions	1 2 3 4
• Consistent, meaningful job reviews	1 2 3 4
• Sincere communication by Managers	1 2 3 4
• Work Life Balance	1 2 3 4
• Recognition for achievements	1 2 3 4
• Competition between groups	1 2 3 4
• Diversity, professional/personal cultures	1 2 3 4
• Social interaction at all levels	1 2 3 4

Does Well = 36

Conduct collective surveys by asking same questions in groups.

- By levels,
- By divisions,
- By location,
- By other group configuration as appropriate,
- By mixing group members with one representative per group

Tally results by individuals and groups.

- Compare
- Chart all

Discuss results and plan.

Lean Perspective

Use Jeffrey Liker's 14 lean principles as applicable.

1. Base management on long term philosophy.
2. Create a continuous process.
3. Use "pull" systems to avoid overproduction, duplication.
4. Level out the workload, work like a tortoise not the hare.
5. Build a culture of stopping to fix problems to get quality right the first time.
6. Standardized tasks and processes are the foundation for continuous improvement.
7. Use visual controls so no problems are hidden.
8. Use only reliable, thoroughly tested technology.
9. Add value to the organization by developing your people. Grow leaders who thoroughly understand the work.
10. Develop exceptional people and teams who follow the company's philosophy.
11. Respect your extended network of partners and suppliers by challenging them and helping them improve.
12. Go and see yourself each project to thoroughly understand the situation.
13. Make decisions slowly by consensus; thoroughly consider all options, voice decisions quickly.
14. Become a learning organization through relentless reflection and continuous improvement.

 Mindfulness – Re-Minder

To tackle your plan of action effectively, practice mindfulness regularly. Recharge your brain, unleash your creativity, and customize your tool kit for healthy body, mind, and spirit. Adapting a lean approach takes time, empathy, perseverance.

8 MONDAY VIP – WORKING LIFE OF IT GURU

Monday, we begin our work week visits by bringing awareness to the working life of our first VIP, Information Technology (IT) Guru, IT Manager, Mr. Unheard-Overworked (Mr. U.) We detail his DYS challenges and suggest steps toward zapping DYS to transform the working environment. Mr. U. works for the Professional Design and Construction, Co. (PDC); a medium sized, privately owned firm, with 65 employees, 20 years in business. He deals with DYS on several levels. His responsibilities involve in house and offsite IT management.

Depending on project load, approximately one third of PDC employees work on job sites in work trailers or at client facilities as engineers, environmental scientists, architects, and project managers (PMs). The PMs oversee PDC staff as well as subcontractors in specialties such as mechanical, electrical and plumbing (MEP), heating and ventilation (HVAC), and surveying. A majority of PDC staff work at the company office in a downtown high rise.

Though most Computer Aided Design (CADD) and Building Information Modeling (BIM) take place at the downtown office, some is done on project or subcontractor sites. Conversely, some project demands require subcontractors and PDC engineers and architects to use PDC's capabilities at the downtown location. Mr. U.'s oversight duties include document storage, management, and cyber security.

With PDC for 15 years, he joined the firm of 16 staff five years after its founding. Before the Senior VP hired him, PDC did not have an IT manager. Mr. U.'s initial responsibilities included software and hardware oversight and repair have grown to include all electronic document management and staff training in IT protocol. His requests for telecommuting twice a week have been denied. He works on site, long hours and weekends.

This time, his call to our DYSpatch ER Center comes ten years almost to the day since our last DYS Virus zapping operation at PDC. At that time, the CORE team included five PDC employees. Currently, the CORE team has four members, Mr. U., two mid-level managers, three years with the company, and the Chief Financial Officer (CFO). After an interim replacement the latest CFO came on board two years ago. According to Mr. U., the current CFO wants to reduce the rising costs of retraining with the increase in employee flight in the last two years. She has a strong interest in the CORE team's success in zapping DYS.

Mr. U. tells us that DYS symptoms returned when the news of reduced public sector funding sent PDC upper management into a crisis mode. Communication broke down; rumors abounded about the response to the reduced work load. Within three months, two senior VPs in charge of client relations and HR respectively, retired early. Three senior project managers left the company to work for competitors.

The prior PDC DYS Zapping operation ten years ago initiated by the VP for Business Development and Client Relations, was triggered by employee and client complaints about mismanaged communication. Communication skills and sensitivity training solved the DYS infiltration at that time.

Our Mission

We need to stem the tide of discontent carrying an exodus of PDC employees to competing companies. Improving communication and HR policies with sincerity and empathy will build trust.

We arrive in at 6 PM, as requested. We enter a mostly deserted office. Mr. U's workday began at 7 AM. His eyes rest on the family photo of his five year old twin boys and seven year old daughter, nestled against him and his wife. "I missed another baseball game, first one for the twins," he sighs.

"They know how hard you work…"we reassure him. His dissatisfaction palpable, Mr. U. continues, "I have just about had it with this job. Nobody appreciates my work. Nobody listens to my suggestions on keeping the software standardized. As we use more and more laptops in home offices and tablets in the field the potential for harmful software and hacking increases. The higher ups give lip service to raising cyber security awareness. Yet they are as guilty as other staff in downloading apps and software without clearing it with me first. They promise potential clients IT capabilities without asking me whether we have capacity to provide such services. And… to top it off I received a bad performance evaluation from someone who knows nothing about IT. I think someone is trying to get a friend in here, to take my place. After all the sweat and sacrifice I've put into this place!"

"Upper management does not set a good example about following my directions. A month ago we had a server meltdown when one of our VPs clicked on a doomsday link that came through a new client's documents. And, I got blamed of course!" He exclaims.

"Are you worried about another melt down or ransomware?" We ask. His harried face signals, "yes." This dedicated employee overrides his desire to be with his family, fulfilling his responsibility to his company. He takes his IT security mission seriously. He, the rest of the CORE team, and we, all share the commitment to maintain IT systems as well as the working environment free of viral infiltration.

"Our Mindful Owl Eyes, independent observers with their methods and tools, will help." We reaffirm. Mr. U. nods agreement. He wants the

DYS zapping and transformation work to begin. "That's why I reached out to you. The other CORE team members work late too. I'll call them in. I'll tap the CFO; I know she wants to help. Let's get down to the zapping. What do you need to know besides the obvious?" He asks.

We tour the office, document visual observations, note locations for follow up physical samples, examine historical data, and share our preliminary findings with Mr. U. and the PDC CORE team. We share our data and interpretations of DYS levels. We review zapping tool specifications for confirmatory Phase 2 onsite sampling. We outline the strategy for Phase 3 cleanup. Ridding PDC of DYS infiltration will pave the way to Phase 4, sustained *OH&F*.

Due to the urgency here, the virulence of reoccurring DYS, we lay out the strategic plan for counteracting DYS efficiently and quickly. Of the most worrisome DYS virus effects at PDC; employee confusion and disengagement top the list. Using an engaged full brain methodology, our plan to zap and mindfully transform this working environment must incorporate input from staff, management, and clients. Take a look at our suggested questions. Feel free to formulate your own.

The CORE team advises that after interpreting results and formulating a suggested DYS elimination action plan, PDC gauge the reaction of employees and management at all levels in an open forum. This welcoming forum will allow for discussion that will improve the plan through inclusion and the sharing of knowledge from a wide range of staff.

After adjustments of the plan to match the lessons learned in the open forum, the CORE team plans to estimate the implementation's success factors over an agreed upon, realistic timeline. The CORE team suggests continuing measurements with honest, detailed appraisals every three months, for at least a year.

Improved Employee Relations

Mitigate Employee Flight

DYS effect – poor communication = mistrust

- Does upper management communicate changes in company's plans sincerely and in a timely fashion?

- What input does the company seek prior to making decisions on changing course in pursuing new markets?

- How does upper management present these decisions?

- What change preparedness plans does the company have in place to ready current staff to transition to new market business development, culture, and demands?

- How do the company decision makers transition from change preparedness to change readiness?

- How often do scenarios occur when decisions seem to come out of the blue without apparent justification?

- How does the company present reasons for the increased rate of unsuccessful bids?

DYS effect – disconnected HR policies = unfairness

- Statistics bear out that employees do not leave organizations, they leave their bosses. How has does the current atmosphere affect behaviors between managers and the staff working in their departments, units, or groups? How do managers conduct reviews of the staff working with them or for them?

- How do employees perceive performance evaluations? Is there a perception of these being punitive and/or as politically or personally motivated? How do employees express this?

- How does the company integrate its HR department into its cultural fabric and employee relations priorities?

- How does the company distribute its training resources?

- How well does the company keep its promises? Does it "train employees for success so well that they can leave while treating them so well that they want to stay?"

- Overall do performance evaluations set a positive tone for encouraging employees to be successful in their jobs?

- How has policy regarding talent growth and employee retention changed in the last two years, five years, ten years?

DYS effect – unprofessional, thoughtless behavior = flight

- How do the decision makers set a behavior example?

- How does the company show employee appreciation?

- What open input forums does the company provide?

- What prevents bullying at all levels?

- How do the decision makers handle unprofessional behavior?

- What exit interview data does upper management use to gauge reasons for employee flight?

- How does upper management integrate employee turnover data into company-wide policies?

- What behaviors encourage lean management at all levels?

Communication, Policy, and Behavioral Changes

The CORE team survey and observational results point to necessary changes in communication flow, human resource policies, and management's behaviors. The sudden decrease in public sector work that PDC relies upon has serious impact on morale and company direction. Upper management decisions to change course toward private sector engineering, design, and construction must be based on input from staff at all levels and from long term clients. The lack of a well communicated course of action creates an atmosphere of insecurity. This in turn causes employee flight, making a difficult situation worse.

The CORE team recommends for upper and middle management to communicate how it intends to portray the engineering and design strengths of its staff to new markets. Clearly lay out plans for training existing staff in understanding the culture of the private sector. Most importantly, involve its staff as PDC's own best ambassadors to new clients. Commit to advancing careers with appropriate skills training all with the intent of promoting success on the job. Create a learning culture. Uphold trust as a key pillar. Trust after all facilitates the mindful transfer and leveraging of knowledge.

Successful implementation – lessons learned

- Adjust communication methods, tone, and flow to avoid rumors and clarify decisions.
- In these changing times when the company has decided to increase private sector market share, strengthen training in understanding the culture of this new market.
- Adjust human resources policies as needed to calm fears of sudden shifts in responsibilities and expectations.
- Demonstrate confidence in change preparedness and change readiness with clear message from the highest levels.

- Demonstrate, real, positive changes implemented by a plan of caring behavior toward employees.
- Encourage team building and sharing ideas in understanding private sector culture(s) in formal and informal settings.
- To add to collective strength, give employees who do not usually work together the opportunity to interact.
- Facilitate a multi-disciplinary network within and outside of the company provide a well-rounded perspective, essential for success for internal and external relations.
- View networks in ways from which all can learn. Younger employees have technical knowledge to share with seasoned professionals running companies. This combined network creates positive internal and external image for new markets.
- Establish cross- generational formal or informal mentoring reaffirming that we all learn from each other.
- Nurture "natural connectors," "natural mentors" for career advice and high level business operations guidance.
- Show appreciation in meaningful ways.

A learning environment leads to a more diverse and wider band of knowledge ready to meet new challenges. When we value perspectives beyond your own we demonstrate our own collective value to others.

A learning, sharing, environment keeps you fit!

 Record your daily, weekly, and monthly routines to build *OH&F*. Mindfully examine them for their effectiveness. Adjust as needed.

Suggested "Routines" to Enhance *OH&F*

Monday   Listen actively and learn from a colleague's description of a fun weekend.

Tuesday   Facilitate mentoring.

Wednesday Take time to listen to creative solutions.

Thursday   Encourage experimenting with new approaches welcoming failures and mistakes as opportunities for growth. Remember the Michael J. Scott quote.

Friday   Delegate tasks recognizing talents better than your own.

Weekend   Play, focus on living the now. Listen and learn.

Weekly   Laugh at yourself every day of the week.

Monthly   Every day, give praise unconditionally.

Ongoing   Take and offer mindfulness training. Practice daily.

Discuss your own routines and those of your colleagues.

- Add to the daily lists.
- Alternate the routines.
- What would a monthly list look like?

Provide a forum for discussing routines that enhance *OH&F*.

Choose a stress scenario to address such as:

- Reduction in new work for the company
- Change in market
- Keeping up with technological advances and tools

Work out the solutions using everyone's talents, including:

- Staff at all levels
- Subcontractors, suppliers, and volunteers who add to the value of your services.

Regularly engage your full brain with mindfulness practice.

- What feels good to do on a regular basis?
- What surprises, what activities that you don't do often would feel good for body and mind?
- Bounce around ideas with family, friends, and colleagues about surprises.
- Make time for a "retreat" for breathing, for meditation, for creativity, for restoring individual balance.

Practicing mindfulness shapes leaders with high EQ and CQ. These skills build *OH&F*, human relationships, and strong structural pillars.

Fill in survey with six key elements that pertain to EQ, SQ, and CQ.

1. When I walk into a room I notice _____.
2. When I send emails I make sure to _____.
3. I am planning a holiday party for staff and their families to celebrate _____Themes and activities will include: _____.
4. Since we have hired_____ there has been a change in atmosphere. I think this is because _____.
5. There is an expected change in project requirements from the technological standpoint. The best way to prepare staff is _____.
6. There is an unexpected change in our economic forecast that will mean changing our market focus. The best ways to communicate the needed changes are by empowering staff in the following ways _____.

9 TUESDAY VIP – WORKING LIFE OF ACCOUNTS PAYABLE MAVEN

On Tuesday, we bring awareness to the working life of our VIP, Accounts Payable Maven, Ms. Trustworthy-Frustrated (Ms. T.) who leads the Accounts Payable Department (APD) of the Municipal Public Agency (MPA). For 12 years, Ms. T. and her staff have provided superb quality assurance for vendor invoices coming in and payments going out. This has kept the project managers from MPA departments heading construction, permitting, and infrastructure work focused on their tasks. Quick turnaround on payments encourages vendors to provide good service knowing invoices will be paid promptly.

Mrs. T. has worked for the MPA in several capacities for 26 years. In the last 12 years she has supervised the APD. Municipal and state elections did not affect her position. She stayed on board during three major reorganizations of MPA's departments. Under her leadership APD has remained consistently efficient despite changing expectations and extended responsibilities.

In the last six months however, efficiency at APD has been undermined by the implementation of the New Accounting System (NFS). The DYSpatch ER calls come in quick succession from Ms. T., two MPA colleagues, and a consultant from Company G who spearheaded the migration to the NFS. The consultant wants to remain involved anonymously via blind copied emails. Her participation marks an interesting twist. We listen and learn.

Due to the rushed migration to the NFS Ms. T. and five staff cannot keep up with the accounts payable tasks. Inadequate training and hurried implementation frustrates their efforts. At the onset of this operation, in addition to Ms. T., our CORE team includes a financial analyst newly hired to facilitate the migration to the NFS, and the Construction Permit Department manager who relies heavily on APD to keep his projects on schedule. He has been with MPA for 15 years.

"Over the last ten years APD's efficiency became a model in the county and region, an accomplishment for all at the MPA. "The agency reduced its invoice turnaround time due to the efforts of my staff." Ms. T. states proudly. She explains how APD enhanced working relationships between vendors and MPA departments such as planning, engineering, and construction, reliant on vendor services.

"Prior to the improvements waiting for months to get paid drove qualified vendors and consultants away. APD's stepped up invoice payment process produced a larger pool of vendors to choose from," she continues. We find out that this suited MPA construction and engineering project managers very well, enabling them to focus on the tasks at hand rather than fielding vendor questions on payments.

In the last six months the APD Department has been losing efficiency due to the poor NFS integration and incomplete training. The rationale for the decision to implement NFS at the municipal level stemmed from the need to match the county's NFS in place for two years. In the last three months Ms. T., her staff, and MPA departments dependent on efficiently processed invoices have shared ideas on how to overcome road blocks. Positive intent to improve the situation and dedication of CORE team members and the MPA staff put up a strong defense against DYS. In this case, to be effective in staving off DYS, we address the circumstances beyond MPA's control.

Consulting Company G. implementing the NFS uses a train the trainer approach. It trained one MPA staff person to train his colleagues. Unexpectedly, the trainee had to take paternity leave shortly after training began. With only a couple of weeks left on their contract Company G. trained another MPA staff with abbreviated content. The second trainee assimilated as much knowledge as possible. According to our anonymous Company G. consultant; with the complexity of the new system, the trainee feels inadequate to train others. Consequently, she is overwhelmed and unhappy.

The public facilities manager anxious to resolve the accounts payable bottleneck convenes focus groups and facilitates individual employee interviews. With the results of these discussions, and data from our cumulus data cloud and DYS Zappers resources, we have a solid base for establishing a strategic transformation plan.

We conduct an analysis of strengths, weaknesses, opportunities, and threats (SWOT) keeping in mind its usefulness and limitations. We go beyond a standard SWOT by involving staff at all levels. Keeping in mind that findings will be subjective and will differ by individuals and groups based on their familiarity with MPA's operations and by their investment in specific operational aspects. The CORE team carries the SWOT data further by prioritizing it, putting it into context of culture and expectations, and formulating realistic solutions that can be implemented within a workable timeline. SWOT analysis findings:

Strengths – Built in knowledge base and collaborative spirit.

CORE team communicates the importance of going beyond the SWOT analysis by addressing subjectivity, cultural context, differences in findings by groups and by individuals. Strategies moving forward will build on strengths with a clear understanding of the data.

Weaknesses – Inadequate training caused by flawed subcontracting vehicle that left Company G. unable to extend the contract for a short time and finish the training.

CORE team emphasizes management preparedness to avoid similar situations in the future. Change readiness would include contract agreements that would insure continuity of operations.

Opportunities – Tapping the wealth of in house and sister agency knowledge as well as garnering support from internal constituents such as the project managers affected by the NFS implementation.

Core team prioritizes opportunities to address weaknesses found. It creates a contact list of sister agency individuals who interact with APD. It implements a plan to tap resources familiar with this NFS.

Threats – Employees unable to do a good job at training colleagues and APD not processing invoices and payments as efficiently as in the past. The largest potential threats of DYS infiltration are behaviors and symptoms such as feelings of helplessness and stress.

CORE team stresses the importance of formulating a change management plan that puts trust at the forefront and employee recognition a constant. APD staff will make this transition work!

Respond holistically to SWOT

The holistic response to the SWOT findings, going beyond data, and the dedication of the CORE team will stop emerging DYS symptoms. We recognize strengths and their potential for contributing toward solutions and actions to fix the situation.

Take immediate action by facilitating communication between stakeholders to counteract DYS impact due to the accelerated NFS migration schedule.

- Formulate and implement a plan to communicate with all the players in this migration challenge, within and outside MPA.

- Establish lines of communication with public agencies whose migration is further along. Share contact information

- Discuss whether the current MPA migration to NFS timetable is best for the situation. Gather knowledge from other agencies that have gone through NFS implementation.

Fix the DYSruption by creating an environment for collaboration and knowledge exchange.

- Build on APD and MPA strengths. List and quantify them in terms of people, planet, and profit. Make them known to everyone in MPA and to MPA constituents.

- Maintain pride in MPA's APD. Document with testimonials of satisfied project managers from various MPA departments as well as vendors. Celebrate the people who created the climate of pride in work well done.

- Recruit allies. Ask for support from MPA departments in requesting to extend train the trainer contract by Company G.

- Identify and use talent in house. Tally the skills in house that may not have been tapped to date for this situation.

- Engage others. Since the NFS has been launched throughout the county for a couple of years, learn from their implementations. Arrange for visits to and from those agencies to tap into their resources. Use their NFS lessons learned to shore up the current trainee's knowledge.

- Praise current trainee at every occasion. Encourage her to continue training of colleagues to the best of her abilities. Link her with other trainers and trainees in the county.

- Plan cross-training to avoid future roadblocks to efficiency.

Implement effective communication methods.

- CORE team members and supporters contact and tap in house and out of house resources.

- Apprise constituents affected by NFS implementation of positive intent to ameliorate situation.

- Set and communicate realistic goals to staff, MPA, and constituents about returning to previous efficiency.

- Seek and incorporate ongoing internal and external input.

Encourage active mindfulness strategies.

- Keep an eye on DYS symptoms affecting engagement within your group and those groups affected by your changes.

- With frequent and unconditional praise improve employees' self-confidence during the NFS implementation stages.

- Communicate often with staff, MPA department chiefs, and vendors interacting with APD.

- Reduce stress by providing opportunities to participate in the solutions.

- Provide setting for mindfulness practice.

 Mindfulness – Re-Minder

Be generous with praise and recognition. Employees will respond with sincere engagement and dedication in their work.

10 WEDNESDAY VIP – WORKING LIFE OF COMPETITIVE SPIRIT

On Wednesday, our third work day, we bring awareness to the working life of our VIP Competitive Spirit Ms. Insecure-Climber (Ms. I.), Vice President at the Small Business Lending (SBL) group of Your Community Bank (YCB). She has worked for YCB for 12 years. We come in response to Ms. I.'s call.

When she worked at a different bank prior to joining YCB, a colleague had told her about DYS Zappers facilitating the implementation of a communication plan at that institution. The results were good. She kept the contact information.

Her practical mind prompts her to form a CORE team and reach out to DYSpatch ER. In addition to Ms. I., the CORE team includes one of the bank's industrial holdings appraiser (Mr. A.), the public relations branch manager (Ms. P.), and a risk analyst (Mr. R.). Kudos to Ms. I. for taking the plunge! She and her colleagues feel DYS presence. Representing several professional and personal cultures, this CORE team wants to uncover and root out DYS at YCB. She tells us, "I hope we can make it work. We don't know how much can be implemented given the state of flux caused by the purchase 18 months ago of YCB by Large National Bank (LNB)."

According to our historical data, when this family-operated bank opened its doors 75 years ago in an urban blue collar neighborhood in proximity to manufacturers and evolving industrial parks, the founders worked hard building a loyal customer and employee base. The demographic changed to a growing middle class with rising incomes from local jobs. The owners wisely predicted the financial needs of residents, industrial enterprises, and manufacturing industry suppliers. With its friendly, unpretentious atmosphere, YCB attracted small factories, suppliers, and retailers as well as their employees. YCB believed in the importance of these businesses. Let us keep in mind that according to current data, small businesses provide half or more of the jobs in the United States. YCB prided itself in responding to their community's financial needs. Throughout its history, YCB specialized in lending to small businesses with $15 million or less in gross revenues.

YCB gave entrepreneurial businesses favorable rates and repayment options, expanded lines of credit, and provided financial mentoring. Most of YCB staff lived in the area, knew their banking customers from multi-generational social interaction. YCB grew to six regional branches. YCB management created a welcoming atmosphere for staff and clients. They attributed bank success to all employees rather than departments. For YCB, competitive spirit referred to competition with other banks, not within their own bank.

Ms. P. explains, "LNB sought a larger foothold in the small business lending market and purchased several privately owned banks with small business clients. Through the rumor mill we have heard that with the YCB purchase LNB, intends to merge YCB with other recently purchased banks. Officially they tell us that during the transition expected to last two years, any merged entity will remain at the same location. LNB will retain the YCB acronym tied to YCB's positive image. Capitalizing on the positive reputation of the several privately owned banks it has purchased, LNB calls itself 'the bank family.' We know that LNB responds to investors, not to small business clients or to community needs. There is a disconnect between LNB's marketing speak and, reality."

Mr. R. continues, "as a result of the merger there has been a shift in culture and priorities. This has quickly trickled down the chain of command. Lending has become increasingly impersonal, with stringent requirements on small businesses no matter their circumstances. I understand this somewhat from the risk perspective. I think though that this new climate does not encourage responding to small business needs. It cuts out our main market base. Lending portfolios represent numbers period. Sadly, customer and staff loyalty have become meaningless from the larger national bank perspective. "

We agree with the CORE team's assessment that the consequences of this change in priorities have already led to DYSfunction symptoms of insecurity and mistrust among staff and clients. Remedies should be applied in quick order before DYS becomes entrenched.

It is clear from our interaction with Ms. I. who for ten years has headed the SBL unit at YCB that she reacts to rumors regarding the possible elimination of her job. The potential merger of her SBL group with two other groups into a single, regional business lending unit in another state has her worried. She must build her portfolio with new loans and get older loans repaid or renewed at higher interest rates. She also must reduce risk by identifying clients whose credit history has been affected by recession trends. She has been told to get those loans off the books as quickly as possible no matter how high the clients' ranking on the loyalty index. The new risk formulas do not take into account how long the clients have done business with YCB – some for two or three generations – and how many new clients the bank gained through their recommendations.

Ms. I.'s experience teaches us how easily DYS can invade a workplace atmosphere. It teaches us how a valued, loyal, highly engaged employee can change in a toxic environment. We learn that her fight or flight mode replaced rationality and fairness with damaging results. The climate of insecurity affected her and her colleagues at all levels. DYS viral infection halted wise decision making. Worry, fear, replaced fair leadership. With rumors running rampant, no one has taken responsibility for action and inaction. With job protection uppermost, anxiety continues to rule at YCB.

Small business owner clients experience firsthand the results of YCB's shift to internal competition and a numbers above all mindset. Behaviors such as Ms. I.'s described below push them to go elsewhere for business and mortgage loans. With this trend YCB's long term clients injured financially through bank staff actions make their unfair treatment known to their own networks. In Catch-22 fashion, this leads to falling portfolio numbers for Ms. I. and her colleagues in other locations. In turn diminished numbers of clients exacerbate staff feelings of insecurity when numbers mean everything. Falling loan numbers lead to increased cross-departmental competition which heightens stress, demoralizes employees, and derails *OH&F*.

During Ms. I.'s fourth quarterly performance review, comments harshly delivered by the new regional business lending manager shook her to the bone. The rumors of merging her SBL group with several in the "bank family" seemed more real than ever. She retells the details. "Unless these numbers go up in the next two quarters," her interlocutor said, "we will have to make changes here. Your group does not meet the nationwide lending, loan renewals, and loan repayment trends." He continued, "If in six months your numbers improve, there may be a regional small business lending unit that you could head. Again, if your numbers justify it." She reveals that for the first time in her career she felt and feels, she is not in control. Leading her current group of three people, one of whom has threatened to leave due to stress, she believes she has little chance of meeting arbitrarily chosen national numbers.

Ms. I. has been a successful ladder climber throughout her 20 year career in the small business lending business. Alone, as part of a team, and leading teams, she competed well against other financial institutions because her attention to small business needs attracted clients to the banks for which she worked. With the merger she finds herself pitted against colleagues in the same institution. At her location she, with two others are the only lenders to businesses under $15 million in gross revenues. Most in her unit have been moved to other locations, or left.

She is now competing against small business lenders in other locations of the "bank family." She wants to keep her job. In survival mode, Ms. I. works very hard to keep lending and loan repayment numbers up in the hope of job stability. She craves recognition for her hard work and would welcome a promotion to lead a regional unit. After her review, increasing her loan numbers uppermost in her mind she began to court clients likely to need larger loans. She did not respond to businesses attempting to rebound from recession trends. Consequently, Ms. I. made decisions damaging to clients such as small business owner, Mr. O.

She called our DYSpatch Center when she realized that her decisions prompted by her sense of urgency to improve her falling numbers caused a diminishing client base. Mr. O's situation brought this home to her. Her insistence in getting her business loan paid first from the sale of this client's home held erroneously in collateral, did not enter her reasoning as damaging to her portfolio numbers. Initially, she did not link her own behavior, to this client filing for bankruptcy, and to the larger symptoms alienating clients.

Reflect on short term profit, long term loss.

Mr. O. has been a YCB client for 21 years, with a business loan in Ms. I.'s portfolio as well as a mortgage and a home equity loan from YCB. Rebounding from the recession, Mr. O. faced a short sale situation. He had never missed a business loan payment and requested that the bank fix an administrative error in loan documents that listed his home as collateral for the business loan. Removing this error would have enabled YCB to promptly execute the short sale of his home and recoup the amount owed.

Mr. O. offered to make accelerated payments and pay off the business loan in two years rather than four. Under this scenario the short sale offer from a viable buyer would have fully paid off the mortgage. Ms. I. insisted her business loan be paid first from the home sale. She focused on the $42K increasing her portfolio numbers of repaid loans. Her colleagues in mortgage loans disagreed.

Inter departmental wrangling between business and mortgage sections and Ms. I.'s refusal to budge on her decision created a decision/indecision log jam. After a five-month wait, the viable buyer walked away. The home sold later bringing in $100k less than the previous offer. This forced Mr. O. to file for personal bankruptcy; a demeaning and avoidable situation. The bankruptcy was approved. YCB got $0 of the mortgage and equity loans.

In addition, the bank lost a loyal, longtime client. Mr. O. "de-recommended" YCB to colleagues needing business loans. He made his dissatisfaction with YCB known to three professional groups on whose boards he serves. YCB's actions became known to community leaders who know him for his and his staff's volunteerism. His well-regarded blog with many followers minces no words to this day.

The real numbers, the $ and the cents (common sense); this customer, long established business owner passed on the word about YCB's behavior. The bank will not regain its $100K mortgage deficit. Customer will not return to YCB. His colleagues, community leaders, friends and family, will not patronize YCB. Should YCB care about short term profit or long term loss? How about LNB, does it, should it, care?

Let's examine this double whammy.

- For customer – bankruptcy filing – loss of business opportunity to bring on investors.

- For the bank – loss of outstanding mortgage loan amount – loss of customers – damaged image of trust and integrity.

Questions to ask when formulating a DYS eradication action plan for this situation – Thoughts on "Competitive Spirit."

- What are the benefits?
- Who are the casualties?
- How to tie internal competition to healthy business growth?
- What mentoring techniques to apply?

Competition – Benefits – Disadvantages

Consider and discuss competition point by point.

- Reasons for pitting one department against another

- Usefulness of an interdepartmental conflict resolution committee to counteract destructive conflict

- Importance of cross-departmental communication and collaboration for *OH&F*

- Open, safe, communication climate

- Purpose of competition
  - Build team work, team spirit
  - Self-improvement
  - Increased production

- Fun and friendly atmosphere brings benefits

- Everyone wins, no one wins, some win, stress

- Essential for people, planet, profit bottom line

- Tied to compensation – how and why

- Tied to recognition – how and why

- When improving and when threatening *OH&F*

- Highlighting and praising talent, progress, and growth

- Benefitting the individual, group, organization

- Tied to job performance reviews

- Tied to job security

- Tied to work life balance

- Expectations clearly stated

- Other considerations of competition pluses and minuses

Write and tell a story about competition with the five endings suggested in *Chapter 2 – Why, What, How, Who*. Can you make it funny? Adding humor would carry a message well.

1. The happy ending with the objective achieved. Everyone wins in this version.

2. Unhappy ending with the objective not achieved. Employees and customers lose something valuable, not measurable only in $.

3. Objective achieved with something else lost. Object achieved and loss could be long or short term.

4. Sacrificing the objective for a greater good; self-explanatory.

5. An ambiguous or bittersweet ending; not fictional.

Mindful SWOT Analysis of Internal vs External Competition

Strengths: The bank's reputation and history in the community, its knowledge of the business community small and large. Note: small businesses provide a majority of the jobs in the U.S. Go beyond SWOT analysis. List, then prioritize strengths. Add a timeline to communicate strength internally and externally.

Weaknesses: Integrating the cultures before and after the acquisition of the YCB – a community bank by a LNB – a national bank. Aside from "family of banks" moniker there is a lack of clear message about the new "brand" for the merged entity, its market focus, and expectations. Go beyond SWOT analysis; list, and then prioritize weaknesses. Add a timeline to formulate, communicate, and implement a solution plan.

Opportunities: Larger network and more resources due to the acquisition by the larger bank. Translating resources into expanding client base and clarifying brand and message. Go beyond SWOT analysis; list, and then prioritize the opportunities.

Threats: Competition overruling ethical behavior between staff and client. Unhappy clients, financially damaged by this bank's changed policies, spreading message of dissatisfaction. How does it affect the triple bottom line of people, planet, and profit? Go beyond SWOT analysis; list, and then prioritize the threats including internal competition.

Thoughts:

- What does healthy competition mean to you?
- What does healthy competition mean to colleagues at all levels?
- Why is climbing a career ladder important to you?
- Who is left behind in your climb, in someone else's climb?
- How is the climb accomplished, at what cost / benefit?

Relationship between Employee Attitude and Client Attitude

Gauge client loyalty and client satisfaction.

Collaborate on designing the best Client Loyalty Index (CLI) and Client Satisfaction Index (CSI) measuring tools for your situation.

Remember that client satisfaction is not the same as client loyalty. Customer loyalty is a long term relationship between client and the provider of services or goods. A client can be dissatisfied occasionally and remain loyal. In most instances, client satisfaction leads to client loyalty. Some of the questions to ask include.

- Is there a practical as well as emotional adherence to the service or product?
- Is the client likely to recommend the service or product to others because the client has confidence in the business?
- How long has the client been using the service?
- What is the degree of client retention likely to be in the future?
- Would the client pay for additional services from the same provider and if so, how much and how often?

Assign numbers to these questions and quantify the importance to the business, institution, or nonprofit.

Let us take this index further and apply it to lean management, where everyone on a team is a provider and a customer. This graphic illustrates the lean manufacturing model, "manufactory" shown here is applicable to all providers of service or product.

- For example in the push and pull methodology of the lean scenario has team member 1 (provider) handed off to team member 2 (customer) what team member 2 needs?
- How has 1 communicated with 2 to ascertain what 2 needs?
- When team member 2 consistently receives what he or she needs to do the job well, loyalty, trust is built.
- How does this work all the way down the line, to staff in the same organization, then to a vendor, to a consultant?

Take on the role of a lean manager. Work to create an atmosphere with reduced stress, increased worker and client satisfaction, better productivity, and more profitability with less waste of human energy.

Below is a lean management of tasks graphic applicable to any size job in any industry, any sector.

Draw your own lean cycle graphic matching your situation.

Since everyone in your working environment circle is both a provider and a customer, empowerment leads to optimum *OH&F*. Empowerment of employees and customers whether they are producing, receiving, or purchasing services, goods, data to move forward with leads to that healthy triple bottom line mentioned in other sections, people, planet, and profit.

Measure employee loyalty and employee engagement.

Collaborate on designing your Employee Loyalty Index and Employee Engagement Index measuring tools.

Express the relationship between Employee Loyalty and Engagement Index (ELI & EEI) and Client Loyalty and Satisfaction Index (CLI & CSI).

Collaborate drawing graphically and explaining the relationships between Employee Loyalty and Engagement and Client Loyalty and Satisfaction. How does *OH&F* affect this relationship?

And the gold medal goes to...

 Mindfulness – Re-Minder

Employees are the organization's most valuable asset. This fact must be integrated into the organization's culture with appreciation for loyalty shown through consistent, sincere communication. During changes employees are the foundation for success in managing change.

11 THURSDAY VIP – OFFICE GLUE EXTRAORDINAIRE

Thursday, on our fourth work weekday visit we bring awareness to the working life of our VIP, Office Glue Extraordinaire, Mr. Loyal-Unappreciated (Mr. L.), Mr. L. works as senior administrative assistant to Ms. E ., the executive director for the U.S. office of Top Education for All (TEFA). Ms. E. leads TEFA's U.S. operations from New York City headquarters. When we arrive, the front office of this nonprofit, social service organization hums with activity. TEFA has as its primary mission access to education in large urban centers for underserved children, in primary, middle, and secondary schools.

Founded 1902 and based in Geneva Switzerland, TEFA has grown from a single office to 18 locations internationally. Most currently, it has six offices in the U.S. In the last two years TEFA has expanded from providing educational opportunities to underserved children ages five to 18, to taking on the role of consultants to colleges and universities wanting to expand their demographic reach. Thus far, each TEFA office in the U.S. and overseas manages the new consulting services implementation in its own way.

The TEFA U.S. office includes four permanent paid staff, three full time, one part time, one full time volunteer, and five to fifteen volunteers depending on activities. Mr. L. reports to Ms. E. She reports to TEFA's International Board of Directors.

Mr. L. and his boss have both been in this office since it opened its doors 20 years ago. Though they do not socialize outside of work they have gotten along well having much in common in their dedication to educational equity. They each have children in various stages of public high school and college education. With the implementation of the newly added consulting services, their relationship has been strained.

The executive director interfaces with donors, "closes the deal," after Mr. L. lays the groundwork with grant writing, outreach, and local as well as national fundraising campaigns. He also oversees volunteer training. They both say that until lately, they have had a balanced relationship, a "marriage of convenience" with well-defined roles. With this balance disrupted, Mr. L. contacted DYSpatch ER.

Mr. L. has been in the nonprofit sector for nearly 25 years. He had gone into education and was teaching high school when TEFA grabbed his attention. He had done volunteer work with inner city children through TEFA and was "hooked" as he describes it. He has a talent for raising funds and making volunteers at ease in difficult situations. In keeping with TEFA's and his personal mission of promoting diversity, he encourages multi-cultural collaboration.

When we visit the office, rings and electronic sound tones of land lines and cell telephones beg for attention. Adjacent to the entrance two bulky PC monitors tightly packed on a brown metal desk, greet us. One of them has a purple sticky note on its black screen "Dead to the World" written boldly in orange marker. A high school aged "resuscitator" sits at the keyboard of the second "living" PC moving to rhythms of the music of his wireless ear bud receptors. "Updating and installing software so that we can respond to the RFPs piling up on my desk," says Mr. L. "Since the addition of educational consulting we respond to RFPs from private and public universities. Chasing after consulting work takes a different mindset and training as does RFP response. Our physical setup and culture do not support this well."

Mr. L. points us to his small office. A colorful outdated music festival schedule held on by yellowing tape around the edges adorns the wall behind his sagging desk. A series of neatly affixed sticky notes in several pastel colors – denoting priorities surround the poster and the frame of Mr. L.'s monitor.

The crammed office has a fold out table tightly fitted into a corner. It serves as a storage area; reams of white paper above and colored paper below, flanked by staplers and hole punchers. Pamphlets and newsletters, sorted in tiered plastic holders. "Getting ready for the fundraising event coming up. " He notes.

A small side office emits the heat and sounds of a large printer churning out donation forms for a fundraiser. This is late afternoon, two volunteers run in from an office down the hall, asking Mr. L. about the hors d'oeuvres to be served at the fundraising event in two days. His exasperation demands quick CORE team action.

We proceed with our preliminary, Phase 1, onsite observation with sampling of physical evidence in the work spaces, the two smaller adjacent offices, and the executive director's larger office at the far end of the hallway. She is out of town, nothing much on her desk, electronic devices turned off. A small printer on a side table sits with a couple of memos and emails forgotten in its output tray. We use our Mindful Owl Eyes tools. The ObservEye 360° Camera scans for offensive language or inappropriately formatted content. We sample for signs of communication etiquette breaches. As we expected her emails contain bold, upper case, red lettering. Ouch!

We pass through the main office to the bustling hub. The Core team has assembled in a corner of MR. L.'s crammed office. It includes Mr. L. along with the volunteer services coordinator Mr. V., and the community relations director, Ms. N. Until recently, Ms. N. had been in charge of outreach to urban neighborhoods, a position that fit her expertise and personality. She feels that she cannot fulfill comfortably the demands of the new "corporate approach" with the added assignment of business development for the consulting practice. As noted, these three and the executive director represent the four paid positions at this TEFA office. Ms. N. has been with TEFA for 15 years. Mr. V. hired four years ago, to handle volunteer outreach, part time.

The CORE team explains that paid staff responsibilities serve the needs of all six U.S. offices. Overworked already they fear the new consulting effort will fall flat without training, planning, and additional staff and volunteers. Paid staff and volunteers wear several hats to fill the gaps as needed for this office and all TEFA U.S. For example, a volunteer reading skills tutor assists with marketing nationally and bookkeeping for the New York office.

Our cloud data provided by DYS Zappers, online CORE team interviews, and preliminary sampling, point to several areas of concern. The executive director, currently at TEFA International in Geneva sends email updates of her meetings, not surprisingly, punctuated in large, upper case, red letters. More than ever, this habit irks Mr. L. and others in the office. This exacerbates underlying dissatisfaction, and DYS influenced behavior.

Mr. L. voices CORE team sentiments, "After so many years of working together you would think that she would respect her staff enough to pay attention to email and memo etiquette. Not sure why, maybe due to stress, she sends more and more inappropriately worded and formatted memos to prospective clients and funders. When we ask her to attend an online class on communication etiquette with us she says she has no time. And... the rest of us have to cover for her, make calls, send apologies.

Over the years, during a crisis, and we have a lot them, she has had a tendency to bombard me and other staff members with improper, insulting, and unprofessional comments." He takes a breath and continues. "Her meanness gets to us. We don't like it. No matter how we either gently, or not so gently remind her about the inappropriateness of such behavior she replies, 'we are one family, and families sometimes have arguments, and say what's on their minds.'"

In agreement, the CORE team members discuss the frustrations with the absent executive director and the shift into a consulting role for TEFA. We suggest that our strategic plan to maintain *OH&F* consider the pluses and minuses of adding consulting to TEFA's offerings, and lay out the infrastructure changes necessary to make this change a positive one for TEFA.

No one questions the integrity or dedication of the executive director, she works long hours along with everyone else. She does not collect a huge salary.

Given that some staff members, two of the regular volunteers, as well as the executive director herself may opt to retire in the next two to five years, long-term health of the well-respected and much needed TEFA U.S. office should be monitored. Succession planning has not begun according to the CORE team. *OH&F* is a necessity for a succession plan to be implemented well. Grumblings, frustration, doubts about the future, insecurity about doing a good job in the new area of consulting, all should be addressed, and, the sooner the better. We all agree; no time for ostrich behavior; time for action.

Open, honest discussions take place as we outline the next steps in reinforcing TEFA pillars, its mission, its viability, and resilience. There are two simultaneous efforts to address. First is the addition of the consulting practice. The second is succession planning. We tackle both with the following surveys.

Importance Chart for Adding Consulting Practice
Score1-4, with 1- Not Important to 4 - Most Important

• Implement training on adding consulting services	
• Address changes in outreach strategies to constituents.	
• Address business development and operational changes for pursuing consulting opportunities.	
• Set up administrative and document management structures for responding to RFPs.	
• Set up financial reporting changes such as audits required for public sector consulting work.	
• Tap TEFA International resources engaged in consulting.	
• Communicate with existing clients and donors informing them of added consulting services.	
• Present the opportunities of adding consulting services to staff in all U.S. offices.	
• Maintain established focus on education for all and assure constituents of maintaining existing mission.	
• Tap staff, volunteer, existing client, and donor resources in all TEFA offices for networking in consulting market.	

• Define consulting services.
   o On basis of current staff expertise
   o On basis of future growth
   o On basis of ROI
   o On basis of market
   o On basis of constituent needs	

• Adjust structure to incorporate consulting.
   o Responsibilities
   o Communication flow
   o Staffing, paid and volunteers	

• Improve current conditions.
   o Clear the air about communication etiquette.
   o Stay on course with mindful, professional, polite, respectful behavior
   o Eliminate meanness factor.
   o Show appreciation for job well done, sincerely.	

○ Discuss improvements openly.
    ○ Seek input from interior and exterior sources.
    ○ Keep track of the group pulse and heartbeat.	

• Formulate a succession plan that includes capturing your internal knowledge and sharing with active mentoring.	
• Implement training for adding consulting to services offered.	
• Address changes in outreach strategies to constituents.	
• Address business development, and operational changes for pursuing consulting opportunities.	
• Set up administrative and document management structures for responding to RFPs.	
• Set up financial reporting changes such as audits required for public sector consulting work.	
• Tap TEFA International resources engaged in consulting.	
• Communicate with existing clients and donors informing them of added consulting services.	
• Present the opportunities of adding consulting services to staff in all U.S. offices.	
• Maintain established focus on education for all and assure constituents of maintaining historical mission.	
• Tap staff, volunteer, existing client, and donor resources in all TEFA offices for networking strategy with consulting market.	

• Define consulting services.
    ○ On basis of current staff expertise
    ○ On basis of future growth
    ○ On basis of ROI
    ○ On basis of market
    ○ On basis of constituent needs	

• Adjust structure to incorporate consulting.
    ○ Responsibilities by current and anticipated staff
    ○ Communication flow	

Add and/ or change categories, tally scores, formulate order of importance and realistic timeline.

Importance Chart for Succession Planning
Score1-4, with 1- Not Important to 4 - Most Important

• Tap resources at TEFA with experience in succession planning.	
• Tap resources in the nonprofit sector with experience in succession planning.	
• Tap volunteer resources for succession planning.	
• Include constituents, volunteers, and staff in the succession planning process.	
• Provide open, safe, courteous, mindful environments for discussing steps toward effective succession.	

• Define positive succession
     o On basis of current workload
     o On basis of future growth
     o On basis of market
     o On basis of constituent needs	

• Address business development, marketing and operational changes during the succession steps.	
•	
•	
•	
•	
•	
•	
•	
•	
•	

Add and/ or change categories, tally scores, formulate order of importance and realistic timeline.

12   FRIDAY VIP – ENTREPRENEUR SUPREME

We arrive in the front office of Creative Print Marketing, Inc. (CPM) specializing in educational materials printing. The summer heat is felt in the office. As we enter a faded photo of a smiling man greets us. The same man, owner of the family-owned, family-run, 38 person company, the CEO and CFO, boss, Captain-Misguided, (Mr. C.), some 20 years older than the photo, barely notices us. He paces the floor. Sweat dots Mr. C.'s face, his light blue shirt streaked with the moisture of nervousness and dismay. He had made the call to DYSpatch ER.

"I don't know what got into the two of them; bookkeeper and secretary, walked out. I didn't say anything today that I hadn't said before. I don't understand it. They have both been here for over ten years. I only asked them for a printout of this year's suggestion box responses. I told them I needed this immediately for the succession plan." His voice fades as he paces.

We observe the four solid, colorless walls that enclose the administrative / accounting / front office. The yellowed photo of Mr. C. is the only adornment. His benevolent smile appears unrecognizable in the current agonized face before us.

"We are here to give the place a good cleaning, a healthy work environment should pave the way for a solid succession plan," we say.

Mr. C. agrees to cooperate fully. He had made the call after all. "Do what you have to do." We quickly apprise him of his responsibilities in this operation. There will be no DYS zapping and working environment transformation without his full cooperation. He affirms, "Do what you have to do."

We know that our DYSpatch ER Center had gotten two calls in the past from Mr. C., four and two years ago respectively. On each of those occasions DYS zapping operation did not go beyond an initial assessment. This third time, the departure of his two long time employees kick starts the push to rebuild, strengthen, and transform.

Mr. C. made the call at the urging of his Marketing and Sales Vice President (VP), Mr. M. with the company for 28 years. They both knew about DYS Zappers when a few years ago a colleague from a professional printers association had told them about our work.

Mr. C. had kept the information on an index card tucked into his dog eared Rolodex business card collection. He passed it on to a close friend, owner of a small accounting firm whose son encouraged him to get his business succession plan in order. Mr. C. had noted how well the succession plan had worked for his friend, a small business entrepreneur like himself. "I'm ready now for you to do the same for me. This time is the right time to get this done for us."" he pronounces in a determined tone.

"We understand," we say. We ask about the whereabouts of the other members of this CORE team, as reported to DYSpatch. Hemming and hawing, C., head in hands reveals that two of the five CORE team members, the bookkeeper, the secretary, his front office staff, had left shortly after he had made the call to DYSpatch. He expected the other CORE team members, the commercial printing manager, Mr. P., and his daughter, Ms. C. Jr., to arrive any time.

"My bookkeeper and secretary said they wanted no part of the succession planning. After they left I contacted each of them by phone, told them I was serious this time. I explained they could help repair whatever had gone wrong before. They declined." He gestures helplessly. "I don't know why…." His voice trails off.

We find out later when we interview them that they do not believe in his sincerity to make any changes let alone go through a succession plan. They do not want to put up with his gruff, impolite behavior. While awaiting Mr. P., and Ms. C. Jr., we proceed.

Assessing the heat index in this windowless room, we stand close to the tiny fan below one of the desks, grateful for the intermittent coolness. We remind Mr. C. that he had made a commitment this time to go beyond the assessment stage. He nods agreement.

We keep our Mindful Owl Eyes 360° Camera activated. While he walks about despondently Mr. C. agrees to our using the DYScover Stethoscope. His daughter, Ms. C. Jr. and Mr. P. arrive. They both give us a nod of approval. Ms. C. Jr. encourages Mr. C. to rest his sweaty body in the bookkeeper's chair, rearranges the paisley cushion on the seat for him. She takes the secretary's spot, props her feet on the step stool beside the trash can brimming with empty fast food packaging. We learn that Ms. C. Jr. will take the Mr. M.'s place once he retires in the next two years. She has worked in the company on and off, in marketing and sales, since her high school years. She has finished a Master's in Business Administration while working at another company. She expresses her wishes to grow the family business.

We get a reading on the heartbeat of this situation. We wipe our DYStrapper treated dust cloth over the secretary's keyboard and bookkeeper's hand held calculator. Our MagnifEye Microscope App runs a quick analysis for the presence of the DYS virus. Data integrated into our mobile device in the blink of a Mindful Owl Eye, calibrate high DYS numbers in this room, with some apparent mutations.

We do not reveal these preliminary results. We are about problem solving, not making DYS virus sufferers feel more stressed.

Mr. C. leaves for a meeting with one of his offsite production managers. He departs with a sigh of relief. We ask the VP and Ms. C. Jr., for Core team reinforcements, they say they will do their best.

From interviews and research we find out that Mr. C., a well-meaning boss has run his company his way, for 32 years. Broad-minded when he started he has become less open to suggestions about adapting to technological and market demands.

- The ER DYSpatch synopsis includes the employee tally.

- Nearly half, 18 employees, have been with CPM for more than 15 years, with four with the firm for over 20 years.

- The sales force of 8 people has had a worrisome turnover rate of over 25% in the last 7 years.

- The production force of 12 people has had a turnover rate of over 20% in the last five years.

According to experts, employee turnover rate should be less than 10%. CPM statistics look pretty good because folder employees have remained on board. Looking at CPM stats closely the picture differs.

DYS Cause and Effect – Symptoms

Employees in the upper management and production ranks at CPM, display a lack of engagement. Sparse training during changing technological times in the industry frustrates them and leaves them unprepared for employment elsewhere. The lack of engagement and technological advancement frustrate newer members of the company. They bide their time, eventually taking flight. The educational publication business thrives on client loyalty. The high turnover rate among the sales force affects sales and the bottom line.

We learn much in this *OH&F* environment. How do we sway this employer change averse to embrace collaboration as a means toward *OH&F*? His daughter, in line to inherit the business needs little convincing. Collectively we must convince Mr. C. to see the value of adopting mindful remedies, incrementally giving up control, and training staff to keep pace with technology.

The landscape must evolve.   Ms. C. Jr. should gradually take on more of the marketing and sales responsibilities. She has gained experience in other jobs and is dedicated to implementing positive changes at CPM. Let's consider the following in mapping our solutions.

Suggested Strategies to Build Muscle for *OH&F*

Explore and document company and industry strengths.

- Long history in the business of print marketing.
- Long time employees have capabilities to mentor.
- Changing technology in the industry has potential to bring new markets to the company.
- Educational materials production has been a growth area in the last few years.
- The industry has much talent to draw from.
- With the blessing of the retiring, open-minded Mr. M., Ms. C. Jr., appears poised to take on niche areas such as online educational materials.
- Mr. C.'s entrepreneurial spirit overrode the fear risk taking when taking on change in the past.

Examine challenges.

- Staff acceptance of Ms. C. Jr.'s role.
- Younger technical staff that brings evolving technology knowledge does not stay long enough to update operations.
- Currently, Mr. C. does not welcome new ideas for growth and changes in technology as he has in the past.
- Familiarize staff with Ms. C. Jr.'s vision for the company.

- Lay the groundwork and communication plan for Ms. C. Jr. to implement change.
- Demonstrate to Mr. C. why and how he needs to sincerely and professionally, and mindfully communicate his support of Ms. C. Jr. and her planned changes.
- Replace Mr. C.'s micromanagement, control over details, with focus on larger strategic decisions.

Engage active mindfulness to bring awareness to:

- DYS symptoms affecting engagement within CPM and those groups affected by CPM changes.
- Changes in the technological landscape.
- Importance of employees as the foundation of success; no economic trends and no shift in market focus should change that perspective.
- Employees' well-being.
- Enhance employee skills to bolster change preparedness and change readiness during transitions.

CPM needs a succession plan to:

- Give Mr. C., family, staff, vendors, and clients peace of mind.
- Provide a dynamic base for years to come.

Succession / transition plan to include:

- Job descriptions for each current position for reference.
- Job descriptions for effective successor(s), not clones.
- Mentoring plan for transition.
- Knowledge sharing, documenting lessons learned.
- Realistic time table for keeping the operation healthy.

Succession Planning Compare TEFA and CPM

What sequence in implementation would you assign to each of these action items? Assume that some will be simultaneous.

What – Define successful succession in the TEFA and CPM contexts. How would they differ, how would they be the same? What universal characteristics can you assign to succession plans in general? Given these two cultures, one nonprofit, one a small family business, discuss and represent visually the particulars for each scenario.

Why – Tabulate the reasons necessary for succession to occur in each instance, TEFA and CPM. Describe the most immediate reasons, and others, perhaps not as obvious. Do this from several perspectives, as the staff, the constituents, and the leadership.

How –   Given TEFA's and CPM's cultures and staff how should succession be implemented? Look for models in similar agencies and similar small businesses. Decide on a realistic timelines that makes the transition as healthy as possible for TEFA and CPM. How would the timelines differ? How would they be the same? How differently would you prioritize the steps toward successful transition? How would you conduct outreach to find a successor for TEFA's executive director?

Who – Decide who could mentor TEFA and CPM in succession planning; preferably resources from similar entities. CPM has an heir apparent, TEFA does not. Who would you tap from another nonprofit that has had a successful succession transition? At CPM should Ms. C. Jr.'s father be her mentor in the transition? What other mentor or mentors would you suggest for her?

Mindfully create a realistic, practical plan with CORE team and facilitation as needed.

- Use your tools and your creativity. A spreadsheet containing each person's characteristics and potential successors may be helpful. How about timeline that makes the transition as painless as possible for the people being succeeded, the successors, staff, and constituents.

- Map out your process verbally and visually.

- Describe leadership skills need for positive succession planning and implementation.

13 ENGAGING OUR FULL BRAIN THINKING WITH OUR EQ, SQ, AND CQ COMPETENCIES

This is our good luck chapter. Gauge your strength as measured through your engaged full brain thinking, individual and collective capacity, your diversity, and the interface between EQ, SQ, and CQ. See the charts below. Ask these questions one on one and in small groups. Each approach has its benefits. One on one interviews provide an intimate climate while interactive group discussions foster healthy exchanges of ideas.

Aristotle said: "Educating the mind without educating the heart is no education at all."

Feel free to customize the tools in this chapter measuring:

- Your trust in your organization, your organization's trust in you, and others' (outside) trust in your organization

- Your trust in your boss or immediate superior, your boss's or immediate superior's trust in you, and others' (outside) trust in your boss or immediate superior

- Identification with professional, sector, and personal cultures

- Cultural diversity as strengths

- Engaged full brain thinking attributes for managing change

- Change preparedness, resilience, readiness, and response

- Communicating unexpected change during a Merger and Acquisition (M&A) scenario

- The interface between(EQ), (SQ), and (CQ) competencies

Questions to Ask about the Trust Factor – Rating 1-4
With 1 – Not Good to 4 – Great

I Trust My Org	My Org Trusts Me	Others Trust My Org	I Trust My Boss	My Boss Trusts Me	Others Trust My Boss
Rating					

Decide how to best tally and represent results.

- Chart the variances of responses by group, department, individual role / responsibility, as well as by professional, sector, or personal culture.

- Present and discuss results.

- Discuss short term interventions and solutions.

- Plan long term interventions, solutions.

Your Cultures – Multi-Disciplinary Professional
Yes, No, Sometimes, Maybe –
Y, N, S, M, Because...

Individual Name (Optional) _____

Do you identify with these professional cultures?					
Identify With	**Y**	**N**	**S**	**M**	**Because...**
Technical					
Operations					
Biz Dev.					
Marketing					
Sales					
Financial					
Admin.					
PR					
HR					
Project Management					
Management					
Org. Dev.					
Training					
Procurement					
Contracts					
Law					
Creativity					
Other					

Your Cultures – Varied Sectors and Industries
Yes, Sometimes, Interested In, No – Y, S, I, N, Because…

Individual Name (Optional) _____

Do you identify with these sector and industry cultures?					
I identify with	Y	S	I	N	Because…
Biz - Small					
Corp - Large					
IT					
Construction					
Engineering					
Financial					
Consulting					
Marketing					
Real Estate					
Nonprofit					
Govt.–Military					
Govt.–Other					
Global					
Public Serv.					
Educ. – K-12					
Educ. – Higher					
Law					
Art					
Other					

Your Cultures– Personal Background and Interests
Yes, Sometimes, Interested In, No –
Y, S, I, No, Because...

Individual Name (Optional) _____

Personally which of these cultures do you identify with?				
Identify With	**Y**	**S**	**I**	**N**	**Because...**
Big City					
Small Town					
Suburban					
Ethnicity					
Nationality					
Race					
Gender					
Religion					
Politics					
Community					
Hobbies					
Military					
Education					
Sports					
Charities					
Social Group					
Environment					
World					
Other					

Internal and External Cultures – Recognized and Celebrated
Often, Sometimes, No, Should Do –
O, S, N, Should, Details…

Individual Name (Optional) _____

Does your organization recognize and celebrate these cultures?					
Org Does	**O**	**S**	**N**	**Should**	**Details…**
Profession					
Discipline					
Nationality					
Ethnicity					
Minority					
Sector					
Industry					
Biz Partners					
Sub-Contractors					
Location					
Community					
Education					
Other					

Mindfulness – Reminder

By focusing and using our senses we hone our emotional and cultural intelligence skills. We bring into awareness the differences and similarities between personalities, cultures and behaviors. We note patterns, refute stereotypes, and anticipate situations.

Celebrating the Strength of Our Cultural Fabric

Engaging Our Full Brain Thinking – EQ, SQ, and CQ – Solid Foundations for Change Preparedness

Essential EQ, SQ, CQ skills for change preparedness and readiness for effective change response:

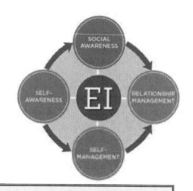

- Four Elements of EI depicted: Social and Self-Awareness, Self and Relationship Management
- Recognition of your own and others' reactions to stress
- Empathy for own self and others stressed by change

foresightguide.com Elements of Emotional Intelligence (EI)

- Call upon strengths of relationships as evidenced in your *OH&F*
- Communication flow that addresses the needs of change response with a variety of if …. then…. scenarios
- Scheduled practices, as for fire drills, in implementing communication flow for change readiness and response matching scenarios, mindful of group and individual cultures
- Operational procedures addressing response that achieves continuity of operations
- Dynamic plan that allows adjusting scenarios
- Active mindfulness in maintaining cultural fabric in implementing preparedness, readiness, and response
- Realistic expectations

A change response plan, with staff and constituents as the audience, presents facts, reasons for change expected or unplanned. It dispels rumors, focuses on group capability to handle change(s). It describes an anticipated course of action, reiterates resilience, flexibility, optimism, and mindfully incorporates feedback.

Tips on Mindfully Communicating Change with EQ, SQ, CQ

- Communicate with staff and constituents often to prevent rumors. DYS thrives in rumor-filled work environments.

- Adapt communication to professional and individual cultures.

- Be mindful of professional and personal cultural differences in dealing with and accepting change.

- Describe the chain of events and anticipated timeline(s).

- CEO, management, and CORE team implementers give a clear presentation of the facts in person to the entire staff.

- Be sincere, honest, without sugar coating.

- Be realistic in your timeline and expectations.

- Detail the reasons for change(s), the challenges, and benefits.

- Commit to maintaining the integrity and trust you have built.

- Implement a response plan that incorporates feedback.

- Using EQ, SQ, and CQ reassure staff, clients, and constituents.

- Focus on strengths; trust, integrity, resilience.

- Welcome the change(s) as an opportunity to work together on a joint purpose, common goals, to grow stronger.

- Be inclusive when discussing all facets of the change response.

- Call on the trust and integrity that you have built.

- Communicate change preparedness, readiness, and response, with concise steps.

- If change affects individuals such as loss or change of jobs communicate with them mindfully, in a timely way.

Scenario and Considerations M&A Driven Office Move

Half of your employees are aged between 22 and 35, one quarter are 35 to 50 years old, and the remaining 50 years and older. Of the latter, a majority holds positions in upper or middle management. They have questions and concerns.

Determine your role – your control.

From conversations with your M&A partner(s) determine how much control you have over the matter, the office design, the staging of the move, telecommuting options, and collaborating with the sister company before the move. Communicate to your staff the details of the decisions made jointly with your Mergers and Acquisition (M&A) partner(s) and your company's level of control.

Communicate change – field questions.

To prevent rumors about the M&A activities, convey to your staff a clear timeline: "In three months, our office of 70 people will move in with one of our sister companies to complete our M&A. The new space fits up to 200 staff. We will therefore have half of our present space. This is more efficient, consistent with our sustainability goals. There will be more opportunities for telework."

Anticipate questions from staff.

- What synergies do we have with this sister company?

- Where is the new space, what are the specifics of the layout?

- What will be the telecommuting options?

- What employee input are you gathering?"

Describe clearly.

- Effect on individual job and departmental functions.

- Expected changes for clients, constituents, subcontractors.

- Timeline for implementing change.

- Steps for mitigating any negative impacts.

- Opportunity for group and individual growth.

- How strengths will carry the group through.

Reinforce your commitment to everyone's well-being.

- I need your feedback now and throughout the process. I am taking full responsibility for making this change go smoothly.

- I will keep you informed at all times.

- Please feel free to contact me at any time.

- We are in this together.

Anticipate team leaders' and managers' questions.

- What training will be provided for those changing tasks?

- How long will we have the same number of employees?

- How will we maintain privacy in this working environment?

- How will we handle confidential material? How will cyber security be addressed if more employees work from home?

- Will we have to pass new security clearances?

- We work in teams. How will we hold team meetings?

- How will we maintain the social bonds we have built?

- What resources will you have for managers to communicate this effectively to their teams?

- Can we have a growth projection so that the managers can tell their teams about the full scope of anticipated growth?

- How do we build excitement about this growth and changes?

Describe the benefits of the acquisition and efficiency of move.

- Explain how the M&A will extend your business or service reach to a wider national, international constituency.

- Describe succinctly how the enhanced geographical reach will affect your business.

- Honestly communicate the pros, cons, and opportunities.

- Make clear how the working landscape will change in terms of essential features such as access, transport, etc.

- Map the processes that with the M&A will give your business and your teams better traction for improvements, efforts, more bang for your work.

- Gather and incorporate input to ensure acceptance.

- Demonstrate that opinions and collaboration matter.

- Reiterate that lean approach puts people first.

As leader, survey your six EQ, CQ, SQ skills and their interface, as applied to competencies – 1 to 4, 4 as best.

Self-awareness – I am self-aware and aware of others in a non-biased way, appreciating differences and commonalities.   ____

Relationship management – I manage relationship by actively listening and responding with care for individuals and groups.   ____

Comfort with ambiguity – I am comfortable with ambiguity and change trusting the strength and skills of staff and colleagues.   ____

Mindfulness – I practice mindfulness regularly and provide space, time, and training opportunities for staff to do the same.   ____

Reflection – I am dedicated to including reflection, thought before action, incorporation of ramifications in decisions.   ____

Empathy – Day to day promote empathy along with trust, ethics, and respect as indispensable for a healthy foundation.   ____

14 LESSONS LEARNED – ZAPPING DYS TO TRANSFORM WORK ENVIRONMENTS

Transform cynical behavior unaccepting of change into positive behavior mindful of individual and group's health. Present honest views describing your boss, and yourself as a boss. Use the charts suggested or design your own. Tally your scores, your opinions.

Map Your Management Flow Charts

Pyramid – top down management, lean pyramid – management supports, horizontal, matrix, vertical flow, circular flow. Draw your own.

Pyramid or Horizontal / Vertical – Top Down Management

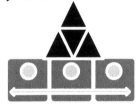
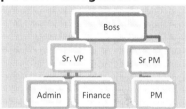

Lean pyramid below – to get the job done mindfully, management supports employees – without wasting human energy and talent.

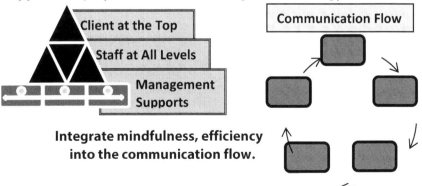

Integrate mindfulness, efficiency into the communication flow.

Commitment to Staff Growth and Success
Always, Often, Sometimes, Never – A, O, S, N
Importance 1-4 from Staff Perspective

Individual Name (Optional) _____

As Staff, my view of my Boss's/Mngr.'s Commitment to Staff					
My Boss(es) Care(s) About and Do(es)	A	O	S	N	Important To Me as Staff 1-4 (4 = Most) and Comments
Well Planned Interviews					
Meaningful Reviews					
Career Goals					
Success on the Job					
Fairness					
Communication					
Integrity					
About Client / Constituent					
Trust					
Mentoring					
Cross-Training					
Work Life Balance					
Sensitivity to Cultures					
Problem Solving					
Innovation					
Creativity					
Sincerity					
Mindfulness					
Community					
Other					

Importance of Individual Growth and Staff Success
To Me as Boss/Manager
Always, Often, Sometimes, Never – A, O, S, N
Importance 1-4 from Boss/Manager Perspective

Individual Name (Optional) _____

As Boss/Manager, My View of Staff Growth and Success				
I Care About	A	O	S	N	Important to Me as Boss / Manager 1-4 (4 = Most) and Comments
Well Planned Interviews					
Meaningful Reviews					
Career Goals					
Success on the Job					
Fairness					
Communication					
Integrity					
About Client / Constituent					
Trust					
Mentoring					
Cross-Training					
Work Life Balance					
Sensitivity to Cultures					
Problem Solving					
Innovation					
Creativity					
Sincerity					
Mindfulness					
Community					
Other					

Positive Work Environment / Atmosphere
Always, Often, Sometimes, Never – A, O, S, N
Importance 1-4 from Staff Perspective

Individual Name (Optional) _____

As Staff, My View of How My Organization Performs				
My Organization Cares About	A	O	S	N	Important to me as Staff 1-4 (4 = Most) and Comments
Change Readiness					
Openness					
Empathy					
People above Profit					
Collaboration					
Ethics					
Planet					
Communication					
Empathy					
Personal Integrity					
Client Satisfaction					
Image					
Mentoring					
Cross-Training					
Work Life Balance					
Sensitivity to Cultures					
Stress Reduction					
Sincerity					
Feedback					
Community					
Mindfulness					
Other					

LESSONS LEARNED – ZAPPING DYS TO TRANSFORM WORK
ENVIRONMENTS

Leonardo da Vinci said:

"It had long since come to my attention that people of
accomplishment rarely sat back and let things happen to them. They
went out and happened to things."

Let's Go Out and Happen to Things!

Adapt to new technology and markets challenge.

Provide a creative space for innovative thinking without judgment.

Use the Six Hats technique developed by Edward De Bono. In this
black and white version imagine the colors. For added awareness,
incorporate the multilingualism discussed in other chapters.

To answer the new markets challenge – each hat has the
opportunity to voice opinion without criticism from others. Once all
hats have had a chance to communicate their positions, a group
discussion follows. Remember the language, role, social sphere,
culture of each hat.

White hat = facts --- Red hat = emotions --- Yellow hat = benefits ---
Black hat = caution, Green hat = creativity --- Blue hat = managing
http://www.debonogroup.com/six_thinking_hats.php

MINDWERX

Dr Edward de Bono's
Six Thinking Hats®

Red Hat
intuition, hunches,
feelings, emotions

White Hat
information available
and needed, facts, data

Yellow Hat
benefits, value,
positive aspects

Black Hat
caution, difficulties,
risks, weaknesses

Green Hat
creative ideas,
alternatives, possibilities

Blue Hat
managing the thinking,
focus, summary

mindwerx.com

Continue by adapting other hats.

The hat wearing globs give you professional and personal cultural insights. What languages does each hat speak? The engineer hat, the business development hat, the sports fan hat, the accountant hat…

And of course your group has its own hats. Draw them. How many do you have, how multilingual are you collectively?

Give those hats a voice, a language. Which hat will collect the data – and what kind of data? Who is under that hat? Who wears the "we can't do it" hat, and who wears "we can do it all" hat?

Now, the talent retention challenge; which hats would you invite into your space?

 Mindfulness – Reminder
Mindful reviews and genuine interest in individual career growth present great opportunities for gaining *OH&F* and building resilience in times of change. Healthy human resources procedures applied uniformly touch everyone.

From experience we know that improving communication boosts *OH&F* in quick order. Implementing communication etiquette such as eliminating red and upper case bold letters in emails and memos goes a long way. Respectful, professional conduct by individuals at all levels enhances the workplace environment.

OH&F Breaks the DYS Cause and Effect Cycle

Individuals structure organizations. They run them.
They work in them. And sometime they get hurt by them.
By eradicating DYS we transform:
Get rid of the hurt.
Cure the symptoms.
Break the cause and effect cycle.
Bring organizations back to health.

Keep Full Brains Engaged – What do you think of this dilemma?

A report required for the completion of a public sector construction project has expired per the regulations and standards governing such reports. To avoid delaying the project a long term client asks the company that has produced the report initially to change the date on the cover page rather than conduct the necessary tests and research to update the information.

What to Do?

Tracing the DYS viral threads – How would you deal with this cause and effect symptoms cycle?

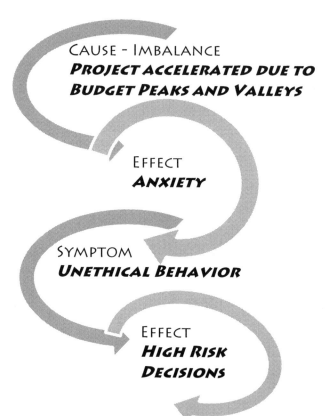

CAUSE - IMBALANCE
PROJECT ACCELERATED DUE TO BUDGET PEAKS AND VALLEYS

EFFECT
ANXIETY

SYMPTOM
UNETHICAL BEHAVIOR

EFFECT
HIGH RISK DECISIONS

Integrity and honesty prevail.

- Remain steadfast in sticking to the regulations and agreements governing projects.
- Cite sources and past experience with similar situations.
- Bring attention to the risk to public health.
- Be a model for and insist on ethical and professional behavior.
- If diplomacy fails, raise the warning flag of potential litigation.

DYS Zapped and Environment Transformed

Take creative and collaborative time to re-visit our five VIPs. What solutions, game plans, does your CORE team suggest? Put on your mindful, lean, engaged full brain thinking, EQ, SQ, and CQ hats!

VIP – Day One
Day 1 – Working life of Mr. U., at Professional Design and Construction, Co. (PDC) – Reasons for loss of mainstay clients partially due to lack of funding for public sector projects – Not communicated well causing perception and reality of unfair human resources practices.

_____

_____

_____

_____

VIP - Day Two
Day 2 – Working life of Ms. T. at Municipal Public Agency (MPA) – New Accounts Payable Department (APD) financial system – Poor training resulting in loss of efficiency and pride in performance.

_____

_____

_____

_____

VIP – Day Three
Day 3 – Working life of Ms. I. at Your Community Bank (YCB) – Small business lending practice culture changed after purchase by Large National Bank (LNB) – internal competition results in unethical conduct toward small businesses that causes loss of client loyalty.

_____

_____

_____

_____

VIP – Day Four

Day 4 – Working life of Mr. L. at Top Education for All (TEFA) – Consulting practice added to existing social service mission – Scarcity of resources and training for new consulting practice – Results in stress and frustration for overworked paid and volunteer staff.

_____

_____

_____

_____

VIP - Day Five

Day 5 – Working life of Mr. C. at Creative Print Marketing, Inc. (CPM) – Necessary incorporation of online marketing services to existing offerings – After 32 years of ownership need for a succession plan.

_____

_____

_____

_____

Engaging your engaged, full brain thinking, collective brains, name and resolve DYS symptoms in real life situations. Try this.

Adopt personality traits associated with the four compass points.

- North: Act – Have a let's do it attitude, to try things, plunge in.
- East: Speculate – Look at the big picture and possibilities first.
- South: Care – Know that everyone's feelings have been taken into consideration and that voices have been heard.
- West: Pay attention to detail – Know the who, what, when, where and why before acting.

 Mindfulness – Reminder

There is never an end to learning new ways of gaining and retaining *OH&F*. Golden rule: in all instances, let us mindfully, actively, champion kindness, empathy, trust, and ethics.

RESOURCES – ANNOTATED WITH DESCRIPTIONS AND QUOTES

The annotated references below, listed by topic include books, articles, and online links with descriptions and quotes in italics. These sources are meant to assist you in formulating your strategic plans for creating and maintaining (*OH&F*). They do not represent commercial endorsements. They are for this book's and www.puliziotta.com website and blog's active users.

In this section I share organizational development and change management classics as well as recent works. Here you find sources on mindful human interaction, full brain engagement, lean management, and details on honing EQ, SQ, and CQ leadership competencies.

Resources included here reinforce opportunities for teamwork toward positive outcomes. They illustrate countless lessons for celebrating human potential. They originate from working and life experience with workplace situations, the input of professionals in several industries, and my research.

I am fortunate to be part of a solid collaborative network representing a variety of professions. I want to express gratitude to my associates, friends, and fellow professionals who continue to share their wisdom with me.

I have wanted to express my concern for regaining *OH&F* in our society for several years. It feels great to have gotten this first guide in a series done. My consulting practice over the last 30 years, existing clients, and colleagues have brought to my attention the public health epidemic of work related stress and disengagement. They have inspired me to communicate our combined knowledge. I look forward to hearing from you, fellow travelers. The *OH&F* journey never ends. Always more to learn!

The next section gives you annotated book and online sources. Use them freely, consult them, challenge them as needed, add to them, and share them. You are the CORE team creating healthy, productive, working environments. You listen, learn, share your knowledge. Our bottom line of people, planet, and profit planet depends on you. Our public health, stress prevention, *OH&F* promotion, depend on you!

Books and Annotated Links

Accountability

Fable based management book by the originators of the Oz Principle, Connors, Smith, and Hickman:

Connors, Roger, Smith, Tom, and Hickman, Craig, *The Oz Principle*, originally written in 1994, revised in 2010.

Online sources on the Oz Principle:

- https://www.partnersinleadership.com/insights-publications/books/
  According to *Partners in Leadership* publications.

  The Oz Principle is the groundbreaking work that demonstrated the vital role of accountability in the achievement of business results and the improvement of both individual and organizational performance. With more than a half-million copies sold, *The Oz Principle* has emerged as one of the most influential and useful business ideas of recent times.

- http://www.huffingtonpost.com/entry/using-the-oz-principle-for-results-in-real-life_us_58cca40be4b0537abd9570e0
  Article on the *Oz Principle* by Glen McDaniel

  The three authors, Connors, Smith, and Hickman, have spawned an entire industry teaching the principle that the trip to see the wizard is a journey of self-awareness and discovery, wherein the characters learn that only they themselves possess the power to fully change their lives.

Online sources on accountability.

- https://www.forbes.com/sites/ccl/2012/02/28/7-ways-to-build-accountable-organizations/#31b752e3cd37
  Article by Henry Browning, a senior faculty member at the Center for Creative Leadership, author of *Accountability: Taking Ownership of Your Responsibility.*   Below is a synopsis of his suggested seven ways of building a culture of accountability

  1. Give clear roles; provide team leadership and individual ownership. Remove confusion. Provide the right environment for learning and accountability by building trust and minimizing fear.

2. Each person should have a sense of ownership for team results. This means each member of the team should feel accountable for improving the process.

3. Most problems have more than one solution therefor each team member should have the support for freedom and control needed to make decisions. Good leaders improve on solutions given by others if needed rather than insisting on their own.

4. Punishment when a goal is not met results in fear and stamps out innovation, taking initiative, and risk taking. Holding someone is not about punishment it's about learning from experience and adjusting as needed.

5. Accountability creates a learning organization that examines what works and what doesn't. Each person should feel confident in saying what they did or didn't do and what he or she learned. Promote a systems approach taking into account internal and external factors, accepting input, and holding individuals accountable.

6. Make evaluation a constant in the organization. Individuals in an organization that stresses input without punishment want feedback to add to their knowledge and become better at what they do.

7. In this atmosphere of accountability integrity counts. Team members who fall short of what they said they would do are called out and they work toward improvement. Consistently falling short of goals may be a sign of low commitment. Low commitment may mean something missing in your culture.

-   https://www.partnersinleadership.com/insights-publications/quizzes/accountability-builder/
    This individual accountability assessment survey has 16 questions with 10 options each for responses. This tool can be helpful in gauging perception versus reality as they relate to accountability.

Change and Transition Management

Change management is a much discussed topic. Below are selected books.

-   Abrashoff, Michael D., *It's Your Ship: Management Techniques from the Best Damn Ship in the Navy*, 1st Edition, 2012.

- Bremer, Marcella, *Organizational Culture Change, Unleash Your Organization's Potential in Circles of 10*, 2012.
- Bridges, William, Ph.D., *Managing Transitions, Making the Most of Change*, 3rd Edition, 2009.
- Johnson, Spencer, M.D., *Who Moved My Cheese? An A-Mazing Way To Deal With Change In Your Work And In Your Life*. 1998.
- Heath, Chip, *Switch: How to Change Things When Change Is Hard*, 2010.
- Kotter, John P., *Leading Change*, 2012.
- Peters, Tom, *The Pursuit of WOW! Every Person's Guide to Topsy-Turvy Times*, 1994.

Collaboration

Online discussion on collaboration includes the following:

- http://epublications.marquette.edu/cgi/viewcontent.cgi?article=1014&context=cps_professional

  Strategies and Benefits of Fostering Intra-Organizational Collaboration, Katherine S. Dean *Marquette University*, 2010

  This 90 page study examines the benefits and methods of encouraging intra-organizational collaboration.

  Quoting the abstract:

  "Qualitative research involving leaders and professionals in a large professional services firm indicate the difficulty of creating a collaborative culture, even when the firm professes its value. The study findings, while supporting empirical evidence add a rich phenomenological component that recognizes the human challenges with and motivations for collaborating in a business environment. Recommendations for fostering collaboration are discussed."

Communication

Communication related books include:

- Patterson, Kerry and Grenny, Joseph, *Crucial Conversations: Tools for Talking When Stakes Are High*, 2002.
- Phillips, Barbara Ashley, *Finding Common Ground, a Field Guide to Mediation*, 1994.

RESOURCES – ANNOTATED WITH DESCRIPTIONS AND QUOTES

Online sources on communicating through meetings:

-   http://www.nytimes.com/2016/02/28/magazine/meet-is-murder.html?_r=0
    On Meetings – how much is too much? By Virginia Heffernan, February 29, 2016.

    "Meetings": The very word is enervating. With the freedom to peaceably assemble so high up on America's founding priority list, you'd think that the workers of the free world would gather with more patriotic vigor, just as we speak, bear arms and pursue trials by jury. Instead, the spirit in which we come together, almost hourly in some professions, is something closer to despondency. Fifteen percent of an organization's time is spent in meetings, and every day, the transcontinental conference room known as the white-collar United States plays host to 11 million meetings, according to research collated by Fuze, the telecommunications company (which might have a stake in publicizing research designed to stoke meeting fatigue). One study mysteriously calculates that the nation wastes more than $37 billion in "unproductive meetings." The statistics seemed borne out by the several meeting-besotted companies I've advised, and I began to wonder if the Manager's schedule suited anyone but tireless extroverts and PowerPoint connoisseurs.

Competency

Online discussions on organizational competencies:

-   http://hr.tufts.edu/employee-services/tld/resources/tufts-organizational-competencies-2/
    In this *Human Resources Organizational Development and Training Guide*, 2016, Tufts Human Resources Department discusses Organizational Competencies. The guide outlines expectations and employee responsibilities.

    Competencies are knowledge, skills, and behaviors that all employees are responsible to develop and apply in support of the university's mission, values, and goals. Tufts Organizational Competencies reflect the values and vision of the university… describe behaviors that are important for individual success at Tufts today anticipate what will be required for the university's success in the future.

The guide continues to describe Tufts competencies as in the following categories: *expertise; interaction with others, continuous improvement, customer focus, resourcefulness and results, leadership.*

- http://www.americangovernance.com/resources/reports/brp/2009/brp-2009.pdf

  Competency-Based Governance: *A Foundation for Board and Organizational Effectiveness* by the Center for Healthcare Governance and Health Research & Educational Trust, Funded by Hospira, February 2009. This report focused on competencies in Board Members involved in health care organizations, has direct application to what it takes to run an effective organization.

  The Blue Ribbon Panel on Trustee Core Competencies was convened in 2008 to build on the earlier panel's work: to identify individual board member core competencies common to different types of boards that can be used to improve board and organizational performance; and to provide guidance and direction for the field in developing educational and other resources that can be used to apply these competencies to the work of hospital and health system governing boards.

  The personal capabilities sought have wide ranging relevance

  Accountability; Achievement Orientation; Change Leadership; Collaboration; Community Orientation; Information Seeking; Innovative Thinking; Complexity Management; Organizational Awareness; Professionalism; Relationship Building; Strategic Orientation; Talent Development; Team Leadership.

Competition – Empire Building and Unhealthy Competition

Online sources regarding the pluses and minuses of competition include:

- http://yourbusiness.azcentral.com/interdepartmental-conflict-9537.html

  On cross-departmental competition and empire building.

  Interdepartmental conflict occurs when departmental managers engage in empire building. This happens when supervisors try to build up their teams by telling direct reports or the company owner that their department is more important than the others. By doing so, they create a culture where employees devalue and look down on what workers in other departments do. This leads to conflict brought on by a lack respect for the work of others. To prevent this type of conflict, managers should avoid putting down other departments and teach employees about their importance in the context of the overall organization.

On unhealthy competition.

While some competition can be healthy in the workplace, it can also be a source of destructive conflict. When departments are pitted against each other by company management, the result is a closed communication climate where employees withhold information from each other intentionally. If one department will receive recognition or compensation as a result of "beating out" another, it's not realistic to expect effective cross-department communication and cooperation. Companies that encourage competition among departments are well served by reviewing their programs and policies to ensure that they aren't set up in a manner that leads to destructive conflict.

- http://smallbusiness.chron.com/advantages-disadvantages-competitive-workplace-16085.html
  While in some areas such as sales competition can be positive in many other instances it can bring negative results.

  Workplace competition is not always positive. It can create unhealthy rivalries that result in workers resenting one another, which is especially true if one person or team always wins the competitions. This can result in a gap between the "haves" and "have nots" that may prove to be unhealthy in internal work relations. Competition can also create undue stress that may actually prove to be counterproductive to some worker's efforts. Some workers don't perform well under pressure and are actually more productive when the work environment allows for a more easygoing approach to getting work done. Fierce competition may also result in a "win at all costs" attitude that may even bring out the worst in some workers.

CORE Team Building

Online discussion CORE team building:

- https://pm-foundations.com/2011/03/04/pm-foundationsthe-core-team/
  Online article by Steve Hart about core teams in organizations, *how to build them and give them ownership over their projects.* 2011.

Cultural Intelligence (CQ)

Books on Cultural Intelligence (CQ) and diverse cultures in our world:

- De Silva, Cara, Editor, *In Memory's Kitchen, A Legacy from the Women of Terezin*, 1996.
- Eddy, William H., *The Other Side of the World, Essays and Stories on Mind and Nature*, 2001.
- Livermore, David, Ph.D., Leading with Cultural Intelligence, 2015.
- Livermore, David, Ph.D., *The Cultural Intelligence Difference, Master the one skill You Can't Do without in Today's Global Economy*, 2011.
- Pipher, Mary, *The Green Boat, Reviving Ourselves in Our Capsized Culture*, 2013.
- Ting-Toomey, Stella, Chung, Leeva, C., *Understanding Intercultural Communication*, 2011.

Online resources on CQ include:

- https://hbr.org/2013/05/what-is-organizational-culture

  What Is Organizational Culture? And Why Should We Care? by Michael Watkins, Harvard Business Review, May 15, 2013.

  If you want to provoke a vigorous debate, start a conversation on organizational culture. While there is universal agreement that (1) it exists, and (2) that it plays a crucial role in shaping behavior in organizations, there is little consensus on what organizational culture actually is, never mind how it influences behavior and whether it is something leaders can change.

- http://m08.cgpublisher.com/proposals/647/index_html

  Management 08 - Eighth International Conference – Knowledge, Culture, and Change in Organizations, August 5-8, 2008.

  Addressing Cultural Issues when Managing Multicultural Construction Project Teams By: Dr. Edward Ochieng, Prof. Andrew Price – *This paper examines the nature of multicultural project teams and their place in the global business environment. It presents a framework for categorizing multicultural teams and argues that fundamental changes have taken place in the globalization of construction projects. It highlights some of the issues regarding cultural complexity that exist in multicultural project teams and argues that, getting multicultural project teams to work effectively across international boundaries has become a major concern. This is difficult enough to achieve where the team is situated in the same office located close to the construction site. But it is much more difficult for multicultural global projects that have a range of diverse companies involved, are widely separated geographically and, that have very different organizational and regional cultures."*

- https://www.aucd.org/docs/councils/mcc/cultural_competency_asmt2004.pdf

The Assessment of Organizational Cultural Competence was formulated by an Ad Hoc Committee of the Association of University Centers on Disabilities (AUCD). The survey tools can be modified for Organizational Health and Fitness Assessments.

In the current environment, many contracts and grants are requiring documentation of activities concerning cultural competence and/or sensitivity, including self-assessments and training. Therefore, the purpose of the instrument is to assist organizations to assess their progress towards cultural competence, both at the organizational and individual level.

The instrument consists of three sections: 1) Assessment of Organizational Cultural Competence, 2) Respondent Information, and 3) Assessment of Individual Cultural Competence. Section 1 is structured to so that it can be individualized to the organization by inserting the appropriate information in the blanks provided; and by allowing respondents to skip those functions which do not pertain to the organization.

- https://hbr.org/2004/10/cultural-intelligence

Harvard Business Review paper on Cultural Intelligence, by P. Christopher Earley and Elaine Mosakowski, October 2004 Issue.

Cultural intelligence is related to emotional intelligence, but it picks up where emotional intelligence leaves off. A person with high emotional intelligence grasps what makes us human and at the same time what makes each of us different from one another. A person with high cultural intelligence can somehow tease out of a person's or group's behavior those features that would be true of all people and all groups, those peculiar to this person or this group, and those that are neither universal nor idiosyncratic. The vast realm that lies between those two poles is culture.

An American expatriate manager we know his cultural intelligence tested while serving on a design team that included two German engineers. As other team members floated their ideas, the engineers condemned them repeatedly as stunted or immature or worse. The manager concluded that Germans in general are rude and aggressive,

A modicum of cultural intelligence would have helped the American realize he was mistakenly equating the merit of an idea with the merit of the person presenting it and that the Germans were able to make a sharp distinction between the two. A manager with even subtler powers of discernment might have tried to determine how much of the two Germans' behavior was arguably German and how much was explained by the fact that they were engineers.

One critical element that cultural intelligence and emotional intelligence do share is, in psychologist Daniel Goleman's words, "a propensity to suspend judgment — to think before acting." For someone richly endowed with CQ, the suspension might take hours or days, while someone with low CQ might have to take weeks or months. In either case, it involves using your senses to register all the ways that the personalities interacting in front of you are different from those in your home culture yet similar to one another. Only when conduct you have actually observed begins to settle into patterns can you safely begin to anticipate how these people will react in the next situation. The inferences you draw in this manner will be free of the hazards of stereotyping.

On relationship between cultural and emotional intelligence:

- http://blog.dwellworks.com/the-link-between-cultural-intelligence-and-emotional-intelligence

On a basic level, all are competencies that can be learned. Both aim to teach new skills and improve one's interaction with others. Both offer assessments, coaching, and training to guide learners in the right direction. Here is a list of the skills EQ and CQ teach.

- *Self-awareness*
- *Relationship management*
- *Comfort with ambiguity*
- *Mindfulness*
- *Reflection*
- *Empathy*

But what is the underlying commonality running through both? Communication. At the heart of both EQ and CQ lies the ability to communicate with others.

Dysfunction

Book on dysfunction:

- Lencioni, Patrick, *Overcoming the Five Dysfunctions of a Team, A Field Guide for Leaders, Managers, and Facilitators,* 2005.

Online sources on dysfunction include:

- http://www.tablegroup.com/books/dysfunctions - reviews the book by Patrick Lencioni, on the five dysfunctions of a team

  The book outlines the root causes of politics and dysfunction on the teams where you work, and the keys to overcoming them. Counter to conventional wisdom, the causes of dysfunction are both identifiable and curable. However, they don't die easily. Making a team functional and cohesive requires levels of courage and discipline that many groups cannot seem to muster.

- https://www.tablegroup.com/imo/media/doc/Advantagethe_five_dysfunctions(4).pdf

  Model of Lencioni's five dysfunctions:

  1. *Absence of Trust* at the base – with the cure as *Go First*
  2. *Fear of Conflict* – next tier – with the cure as *Mine for Conflict*
  3. *Lack of Commitment* – third tier – with the cure as *Force Clarity and Closure*
  4. *Avoidance of Accountability* – next to last tier – with the cure as *Confront Difficult Issues*
  5. *Inattention to Results* – Top of pyramid – with the cure as *Focus on Collective Results*

- https://www.americanexpress.com/us/small-business/openforum/articles/7-signs-your-culture-is-dysfunctional/

  This article by Alexandra Levit written in 2012 explores the seven signs of a dysfunctional culture - *Here's how to know when your business is going in the wrong directions.*

  1. *Your internal competition is worse than your external competition – this is disastrous for morale.*

2. *Management refuses to change with the times. Darwin said we must adapt or die. Leaders should recognize obvious and sensible solutions.*

3. *You have lost 20 percent of your workforce to voluntary turnover, and you haven't replaced anyone.*

4. *The 'stories from the trenches' are legendary.' If workplace negative anecdotes are many, it is time to replace them.*

5. *Direction from the top is flavor of the week. Strategy changes with the latest management or culture fads. Reorganizations cause mass confusion.*

6. *Bureaucracy reigns supreme. If approval cycles are too long, involving too many people, time to rethink them.*

7. *Innovation isn't really valued. Values about innovation and creative thinking touted publicly should match with what happens at work.*

Electronic Age

Books on technological changes provide a wide perspective on how these changes affect workplaces day to day.

- Belew, Shannon, *The Art of Social Selling, Finding and Engaging Customers on Twitter, Facebook, LinkedIn, and Other Social Media*, 2014.
- Dickson, Paul, *The Official Rules and Explanations, The Original Guide to Surviving the Electronic Age with Wit, Wisdom, and Laughter*, 1999.
- Kawasaki, Guy, *Enchantment, The Art of Changing Hearts, Minds, and Actions,* 2011.
- Tapscott, Don, *Grown Up Digital, How the Net Generation Is Changing Your World*, 2009.

Emotional Intelligence (EQ) or (EI)

Books on Emotional Intelligence:

- Bradberry, Travis, Greaves, Jean, and Lencioni, Patrick, *Emotional Intelligence 2.0*, 2009.
- Cornwall, Michael, Go Suck A Lemon, Strategies for Improving Your Emotional Intelligence, 2012.
- Siegel, Jeanne, Ph.D., *The Language of Emotional Intelligence: The Five Essential Tools for Building Powerful and Effective Relationships*, 2008.

RESOURCES – ANNOTATED WITH DESCRIPTIONS AND QUOTES

- Walton, David, Dr., Emotional *Intelligence, A Practical Guide, Self-Knowledge, Managing Your Emotions, Understanding Others*, 2015.

Online resources on emotional intelligence and leadership:

- http://www.ihhp.com/meaning-of-emotional-intelligence
  Emotional Intelligence (EQ or EI) a term created by two researchers Peter Salavoy and John Mayer and popularized by Dan Goleman in his 1996 book of the same name.

  > *Recognize, understand, and manage your own emotions, and recognize, understand, and influence the emotions of others.*

- https://www.kqed.org/mindshift/40880/a-simple-exercise-to-strengthen-emotional-intelligence-in-teams\
  Four compass points is a suggested team game on this website. The personality traits associated with the four points are
  North: Acting – "Let's do it;" Likes to act, try things, plunge in.
  East: Speculating – likes to look at the big picture and the possibilities before acting.
  South: Caring – likes to know that everyone's feelings have been taken into consideration and that their voices have been heard before acting.
  West: Paying attention to detail —likes to know the who, what, when, where and why before acting.

- *https://liveboldandbloom.com/02/self-awareness-2/emotional-intelligence-workplace*

  > *Emotional intelligence isn't necessary just for senior executives. It's necessary for success at any level in your career. Organization that value emotional intelligence look for employees with high EQ's in order to promote from within and groom for leadership roles. If you want to rise to higher levels of responsibility in your job, having a strong EQ is essential.*

- https://www.psychologytoday.com/basics/emotional-intelligence
- Article in Psychology Today defines emotional intelligence (EQ):
  1. *The ability to harness emotions and apply to thinking and problem solving.*
  2. *Managing emotions by regulating our own emotions.*
  3. *Cheering up and calming other people.*

Employee Relations

Books on human resource management include:

- Nelson, Bob, *1001 Ways to Reward Employees, Money Isn't Everything*, 1994.
- Nelson, Bob, *1001 Ways to Energize Employees, Thank God It's Monday!*, 1997.
- Stewart, Thomas, *Intellectual Capital, The New Wealth of Organizations*, 1997.

Online discussions on human resources:

- https://www.shrm.org/resourcesandtools/hr-topics/employee-relations/pages/default.aspx
  Society for Human Resource Management Definition
    Employee relations mean an organization's efforts to manage relationships between employers and employee. Good employee relations programs provide fair and consistent treatment to all employees. This results in engaged employees committed to their jobs and loyal to the company.
- https://disneyinstitute.com/courses/?CMP=BAC-CRT|9219498|1343251|125224575|0
  Description of Walt Disney Company as a good organization to work for.
    For 60 years, The Walt Disney Company has perfected the art of making people happy. And when it comes to understanding how we perfected that customer experience, well, we think we offer you the most amazing classroom in the world. With courses offered by Disney Institute, you'll discover ways to positively impact your organization and the customers you serve as you're immersed in leadership, service and employee engagement.

Ethics

Ethics in management book:

- Fredrickson, George H. and Ghere Rickard K., *Ethics in Public Management*, 2005 – also available as e-book.

Excellence

Online discussion on excellence:

- http://www.mwsug.org/proceedings/2012/BI/MWSUG-2012-BI05.pdf

Developing an Analytics Center of Excellence (Or The Care and Feeding of Magical Creatures) – paper by Charles D. Kincaid, Experis Business Analytics Practice, Portage, MI

Excerpt on *What is excellence?*

> *The history of this question goes back over two millennia. Aristotle is quoted as saying "We are what we repeatedly do. Excellence, then, is not an act but a habit." Lao Tzu is to have said "The supreme excellence is not to win a hundred victories in a hundred battles. The supreme excellence is to subdue the armies of your enemies without even having to fight them.*
>
> *More recently, Senator Jerry Moran said "Perfection has to do with the end product, but excellence has to do with the process." As we'll see, analytical excellence will come from building a team that makes a habit of strong analytical, business and development processes in order to work with rather than fight against the business.*

Image

Online discussion on image:

- http://www.emeraldinsight.com/researchregister
  http://www.emeraldinsight.com/0268-3946.htm
  The Emerald Research Register and full text archive of this journal are available.
  Eran Vigoda-Gadot, Hedva Vinarski-Peretz and Eyal Ben-Zion, *Politics and image in the organizational landscape An empirical examination among public sector employees*, Department of Political Science, The University of Haifa, Mount Carmel Haifa, Israel. Scholarly articles for Keywords Organizational politics, Organizational profiles, Job analysis, Public sector organizations, 2003.

Innovation and Creativity

Books from multi-disciplinary perspectives.

- Buffett, Mary and Clark, David, *The Tao of Warren Buffet, Warren Buffet's Words of Wisdom*, 2006.
- Burkus, David, *Under New Management, How Leading Organizations Are Upending Business as Usual*, 2016.

- Lynch, James M., *The Hamlet Secret: A Self-Directed (Shakespearean) Workbook for Living a Passionate, Joy-Filled Life*, 2009.
- Gallway, W. Timothy, *The Inner Game of Tennis*, 1997.
- Kleon, Austin, *Steal Like an Artist, 10 Things Nobody Told You About Being Creative*, 2012.
- Pressfield , Steven, *The War of Art: Break Through the Blocks and Win Your Inner Creative Battles*, 2002.
- Tharp, Twyla, with Mark Ryder, *The Creative Habit, Learn IT and Use It for Life*, A Practical Guide, 2003.

Landscape and Geography

Online sources on organizational landscape and geography:

- http://www.innovationexcellence.com/blog/2015/10/07/rapid-pace-change-in-organizational-landscape/
  Rapid Pace Change in Organizational Landscape, Posted October 7, 2015, Rodrigo Canales Ph.D., and Kim Sykes.
  Building Your Innovation Capability: Will you ask the right questions?
  Introductory Paragraph:

  In just the past five years alone, we can see how much the landscape in which current organizations are operating is changing at a rapid pace. Written by Rodrigo Canales, PhD, an Associate Professor of Organizational Behavior at the Yale School of Management, studies how organizations can build a powerful innovation capacity in response to these market forces.

  We can see how much the landscape is changing when we look at the speed with which the boundaries between sectors have eroded. Even 5 or 10 years ago, the boundary between a for profit company and nonprofit company were much clearer than they are now.

- http://www.geo.uzh.ch/fileadmin/files/content/abteilungen/so/Publications_Martin/Mueller_2013_The_Geography_of_Organizations.pdf
  Author links martin@martin-muller.net - www.martin-muller.net
- *Geography of Organizations*, to be published in: International Encyclopedia of the Social and Behavioral Sciences. Second edition. James D. Wright (editor). Elsevier: Amsterdam. 2015. *Martin Müller* University of Zurich, Winterthurer str. 190, 8057 Zürich, Switzerland.

The geography of organization denotes the interdisciplinary study of the spatial aspects of organizations and processes of organizing. Geography as well as organization and management studies are the major fields to contribute to this area. Three major strands of research can be distinguished. One focuses on 'organizations in space' and how organizational action transforms space and vice versa. The second one looks inside organizations and is interested in how space shapes organizational life. The third one moves away from the organization as an entity but rather centers on how processes of organizing create emergent socio material orders

Leadership

Below are some of the many books on the larger topic of leadership:

- Charan, Ram, Drotter, Stephen, and Noel, James, *The Leadership Pipeline: How to Build the Leadership Powered Company*, 2011.
- DePree. Max, *Leadership Is An Art*, 1989.
- Covey, Stephen, R., *The 7 Habits of Highly Effective People: Powerful Lessons in Personal Change*, 1989, 2005 Audio, CD 2012.
- Iacocca, Lee, *Where Have All the Leaders Gone?* 2007.
- MacKenzie, Gordon, *Orbiting The Giant Hairball, A Corporate Fool's Guide to Surviving with Grace*, 1985.
- Simon, Hermann and Zatta, Danilo, *Aforismi per il Manager, Le Migliori Citazione per Ogni Occasione*, [*Aphorisms for Managers, Best Quotes for All Occasions*], 2011.
- Whyte, David, *The Heart Aroused, Poetry and Preservation of the Soul in Corporate America*, 1996.
- Wood, Jake, *Take Command, Lessons in Leadership, How to Be a First Responder in Business*, 2014.

Online sources discussing leadership:

- http://www.groco.com/readingroom/bus_goodleader.aspx
  This website lists and discusses seven qualities of a good leader:
  1. Character - *A good leader has an exemplary character. It is of utmost importance that a leader is trustworthy to lead others.*
  2. Enthusiastic - Good *leaders are enthusiastic about their work or cause and also about their role as leader. People will respond more openly to a person of passion and dedication.*

3. Confident - *A good leader is confident. In order to lead and set direction a leader needs to appear confident as a person and in the leadership role. Such a person inspires confidence in others and draws out the trust and best efforts of the team to complete the task well.*

4. Purposeful - A *leader also needs to function in an orderly and purposeful manner in situations of uncertainty.*

5. Calm - *Good leaders are tolerant of ambiguity and remain calm, composed and steadfast to the main purpose. Storms, emotions, and crises come and go.*

6. Analytical - *A good leader as well as keeping the main goal in focus is able to think analytically. Not only does a good leader view a situation as a whole, but is able to break it down into sub parts for closer inspection.*

7. Excellence - *A good leader is committed to excellence. Second best does not lead to success. The good leader not only maintains high standards, but also is proactive in raising the bar in order to achieve excellence in all areas*

Adaptive Leadership

Books on adaptive leadership include:

- Heifetz, Ronald and Linsky, Marty, *The Practice of Adaptive Leadership: The Tactics for Changing Your Organization and the World*, 2009.
- Heifetz, Ronald and Linsky, Marty, *Leadership on the Line, with a New Preface; Staying Alive Through the Dangers of Change*, 2017. y Ronald Heifetz Heife

Command and control vs people centered leadership discussion:

- http://stephenjgill.typepad.com/performance_improvement_b/2010/05/commandandcontrol-leadership-vs-peoplecentered-leadership.html *Command-and-Control Leadership vs. People-Centered Leadership*, Steven J. Gill, 2010.

   Command-and-control is not always counter-productive. However, many managers in positions of authority will try to control schedules (e.g., time in the office), output (e.g., number of sales calls), and budget (e.g., line item for travel) before they have earned the trust of their employees. So at the same time that they are trying to control everything they can, they say they want employees to be creative and innovative and to respond rapidly to marketplace changes. … people won't be creative, innovative, and responsive, and they won't stay in their jobs, if they feel disrespected and distrusted by their managers. Leaders can't have it both ways.

Online discussion of dictatorial leadership:
- http://www.bbc.com/capital/story/20160310-how-to-tame-the-office-dictator?ocid=ww.social.link.email
  BBC – *Capital Magazine - How to tame the office dictator*, 11 March 2016

   They're know-it-alls and braggarts. They rule with an iron fist. It's their way, their idea, their direction — or nothing at all.

   No doubt we've all encountered a dictator boss, or one with so little humility, we're really not sure they had any to begin with. Is there any way to tame these characters at the office? It's a topic several LinkedIn Influencers weighed in on this week. Here's what two of them said.

   Daniel Goleman, co-director of the Consortium for Research and Emotional Intelligence in Organizations and co-founder of the Collaborative for Academic, Social, and Emotional Learning

   Is there any hope for a dictatorial leader? Goleman tells the story of a manager named Allen. Behind his back, his "staff called him 'Mr. My Way or the Highway'… Allen ruled his department with an iron fist, making every decision big and small with little input from others." Allen's staff didn't dare make suggestions, he wrote in his post How to Coach a Dictatorial Leader.

   Changing a dictator's style only starts with understanding why they behave that way.

   With so much evidence showing that dictator leaders negatively impact team performance, it's not just a personality problem. Executive coaches say dictatorial leaders can be tamed, sometimes. Goleman cited the work of Daniel Siegel, author of Mindsight and executive coach and speaker who tries to understand what makes a person a dictator leader.

   According to Siegel, people need three "S's": To be seen, to be soothed, and to be safe. "When you're safe, soothed and seen in a reliable way, you get the fourth S, security."

The bottom line, Goleman wrote, is that when people don't have these three S's, they lack a sense of security, a state of mind that can make them prone to acting like a dictator in an organization.

Lean Management

Books on lean approaches to manufacturing and leadership:

- Liker, Jeffrey, K. Dr., *The Toyota Way*: *14 Management Principles from the World's Greatest Manufacturer*, 2004.
- Liker, Jeffrey, K. Dr., Trachilis, George, *Developing Lean Leaders at All Levels, A Practical Guide,* 2016. This book includes chapters on learning to coach and develop others and creating vision and aligning goals.
- Seiler, *Rich, The Pull Planning Playbook for Foremen and Superintendents – Learn the X's and O's to Pull Like the Pros*, 2019. In this extensive hands-on guide Rich Seiler Chief Improvement Officer at Unified Works Inc., takes projects from planning through construction following lean principles.

Learning Organization

Learning organization book:

- Senge, Peter M., *The Fifth Discipline, The Art & Practice of The Learning Organization*, 1990.

Mindfulness in Organizations, Employee Well-Being and Organizational Health

Many books have been written since the 1990's when mindfulness was introduced into the workplace by Jon Kabat-Zinn. Below are a few with discussions including the link between mindfulness, employee well-being, and organizational health.

- Chapman Clarke, Margaret, Editor, *Mindfulness in the Workplace, An Evidence-based Approach to Improving Wellbeing and Maximizing Performance*, 2016.
- *Goleman, Daniel, Davidson, Richard J., Altered Traits, Science Reveals Ho Meditation Changes Your Mind, Brain, and Body, 2017.*
- Kabat-Zinn, Jon, *Full Catastrophe Living*, 1990; *Coming to Our Senses*, 2005; Adventures in Mindfulness; 2012.

Mindfulness has become accepted in the corporate sector because of positive data made available through scientific research on the physical and mental benefits of mindfulness practice

- Reb, Jochen, Atkins, Paul W. B., Editors, *Mindfulness in Organizations, Foundations, Research, and Applications*, 2015.
- Watt, Tessa, *Mindfulness A Practical Guide*, 2012.

Online resources, university dissertation, and discussions on mindfulness in the workplace include the following:

- http://acumen.lib.ua.edu/u0015/0000001/0000269/u0015_0000001_0000269.pdf

  Williams, Barry, Wyatt, *Organizational Health and Mindfulness as Predictors of School Effectiveness: Using the Balanced Scorecard* Dissertation submitted in partial fulfillment of the requirements for degree of Doctor of Education in the Department of Education in the in the Graduate School of the University of Alabama, Tuscaloosa, Alabama, 2010.

  Mindfulness is accurately defined as the continuing scrutiny present is some organizations today (Weick & Sutcliffe, 2001). While mindless organizations have a tendency to focus on success and run the risk of growing complacent, mindful organizations not only anticipate problems, they actively look for them. "Mindfulness is a paradox of sorts: it sees problems as opportunities and views successes as problematic; it is both optimistic and skeptical" (Hoy, 2003, p. 97). Problems are viewed as opportunities for growth in mindful organizations. Mindfulness is said to be high in highly reliable organizations (HROs) (Weick & Sutcliffe, 2001). HROs exhibit five distinct characteristics. They are a preoccupation with failure, a reluctance to simplify, sensitivity to operations, a deep commitment to resilience in the face of adversity, and deference to front line expertise in the event of crisis. Page 17.

- http://dx.doi.org/10.5465/amle.2011.0002C

  Vogus Timothy J., Vanderbilt University and Sutcliffe, Kathleen, M. University of Michigan, Organizational mindfulness and Mindful Organizing: A Reconciliation and Path Forward, from *Academy of Management Learning & Education*, 2012, Vol. 11, No. 4, 722–735.

Regarding Ray, Baker, and Plowman's (2011) study of organizational mindfulness, Ray and colleagues (2011) characterize organizational mindfulness as strategic, top-down, and enduring.

- https://hbr.org/2015/01/mindfulness-can-literally-change-your-brain
  Mindfulness Can Literally Change Your Brain, Harvard Business Review, by Christina Congleton, Britta K. Hölzel, and Sara W. Lazar 2015.

  The business world is abuzz with mindfulness. But perhaps you haven't heard that the hype is backed by hard science. Recent research provides strong evidence that practicing non-judgmental, present moment awareness (a.k.a. mindfulness) changes the brain, and it does so in ways that anyone working in today's complex business environment, and certainly every leader, should know about.

Organizational Health

Organizational health has been recognized as an important element for successful organizations. Books include:

- Lencioni, Patrick, *The Advantage, Why Organizational Health Trumps Everything Else in Business,* 2012.
- Lowe, Graham, *Creating Healthy Organizations, How Vibrant Workplaces Inspire Employees to Achieve Sustainable Success,* 2010.
- Stanford, Naomi, *Organizational Health: An Integrated Approach to Building Optimum Performance,* 2012.

Online resources and McKinsey literature and studies include.

- http://www.mckinsey.com/business-functions/organization/our-insights/organizational-health-the-ultimate-competitive-advantage, in McKinsey & Company Quarterly, June 2011, See Chapter *1* quotes.

  Getting and staying healthy involves tending to the people-oriented aspects of leading an organization, so it may sound "fluffy" to hard-nosed executives raised on managing by the numbers. But make no mistake: cultivating health is hard work.

- http://www.mckinsey.com/business-functions/organization/our-insights/the-hidden-value-of-organizational-health-and-how-to-capture-it , McKinsey & Company, Quarterly, April 2014, See Quotes in Chapter 1.

  When we compared the health metrics of more than 270 publicly traded companies with their financial-performance metrics, we found that the healthiest generated total returns to shareholders that were three times higher than those of companies in the bottom quartile and over 60 percent higher than those of companies with "middle of the road" health profiles.

- http://www.acec.org/calendar/calendar-webinars/are-you-building-muscle-or-just-getting-fat/

  Are You Building Muscle or Just Getting Fat? How to Develop Sustainable, Profitable Growth for Your Firm - Webinars on healthy companies by the American Council of Engineering Companies.

- http://www.forbes.com/sites/jeffboss/2015/09/09/organizational-health-or-organizational-fitness/print/

  Organizational fitness is a function of multiple factors: a company's collective performance and how well they respond to an employee's need for meaningful work, how much opportunity exists for personal and professional growth, how well different corporate functions fuse together to share the same purpose, and the difference you make as a leader. By Jeff Boss, who was a Navy Seal – from his book *Navigating Chaos: How to Find Certainty in Uncertain Situations.*

- http://www.mckinseysolutions.com/solutions/organizational-health-index.aspx

  McKinsey Organizational Healthy Indices OHI for several industries includes a comprehensive health assessment to help organizations build a customized road map to enhance long-term performance. Distinct modules provide flexibility to customize health management to an organization's evolving needs.

  The OHI Solution enables organizations to Measure health using an online survey to diagnose strengths and weaknesses.

  Define 'signature' combinations of health management practices and prioritize key areas for improvement.

  Develop interventions and define road maps in action-planning workshop(s).

  Implement targeted actions to improve health in key areas.

  Embed health optimization into performance management cycles through 'pulse checks' and interactive course correction sessions.

- http://www.mckinseysolutions.com/case-studies.aspx
  Industries with OHI results – Chemical, Consumer Goods – Beverages – Automotive
- http://www.ashhra.org/conference/2014/learningsessions2014/M12a.pdf
  In a Health Care Study for the American Society for Health Care Human Resources - ASHHRA – McKinsey describes methods to gauge the Organizational Health Index (OHI). The 2014 conference report includes results of *Surveys* and suggested *Recipes for Organizational Health*.

Productivity and Efficiency

Books discussing productivity and efficiency.
- Babauta, Leo, *Zen To Done: The Ultimate Simple Productivity System*, 2011.
- Carter, Willie L., *Process Improvement Administrative Departments, the Key to Achieving Internal Customer Satisfaction*, 2008.

Online sources and discussions include.
- http://www.nytimes.com/2016/02/28/magazine/failure-to-lunch.html
  NY Times article on trends in eating in the office, by Malia Wollan, February 28, 2016.

  Now some 62 percent of professionals say they typically eat lunch at their desks, a phenomenon that social scientists have begun calling "desktop dining." Eating takes a back seat to meetings, catching up on to-dos or responding to email. Roughly half of American adults eat lunch alone. In research from the Hartman Group, many so-called millennial wage earners said they actually preferred eating solo. A quarter of those surveyed agreed with the statement "I eat alone to multitask better."

  Beyond any health risks, the desk lunch detracts from our sense of the office as a collaborative, innovative, sociable space. It is hard to foster that feeling when workers eat single serving yogurt alone, faces lit in the monochrome blue of their computer screens. Brian Wansink, a professor and the director of Cornell University's Food and Brand Lab, points out that desktop dining isn't even a sign of industriousness anymore; these days, a desk luncher is as likely as not to be scrolling through Facebook. Wansink and other researchers did a survey of fire-department captains and lieutenants in a major American city. They found significant positive correlations between work performance and eating and cooking as a team.

Firehouses where firefighters ate together reported more cooperative behavior; they were better at their jobs.

"Workplace satisfaction is so much higher if you eat with your colleagues," Wansink told me. "You like your job more — and you like your colleagues better."

Respect
Online discussion in BBC Capital Magazine on respect.

- http://www.bbc.com/capital/story/20160304-what-to-do-when-nicknames-go-too-far-at-work?ocid=ww.social.link.email
  BBC - *Capital Magazine - What to do when nicknames go too far at work?* By Angela Henshall, 5 March 2016,

Small Businesses
Online discussion regarding small businesses:

- https://www.sba.gov/sites/default/files/FAQ_Sept_2012.pdf
  Small firms accounted for 64 percent of the net new jobs created between 1993 and 2011 (or 11.8 million of the 18.5 million net new jobs). Since the latest recession, from mid-2009 to 2011, small firms, led by the larger ones in the category (20-499 employees), accounted for 67 percent of the net new jobs.

Social Intelligence (SQ)
Books on social intelligence

- Riggio, Ronald, E., Murphy, Susan, Pirozzolo, Francis, *Multiple Intelligences and Leadership*. 2002. Chapter 3 specifically addresses Social Intelligence.
- Goleman, Daniel, Dr., *Social Intelligence: The New Science of Human Relationships*, 2007.
  https://www.scienceofpeople.com/social-intelligence/ Vanessa Van Edwards in Science of People recaps Goleman's findings. Her recap includes the High Road and Low Road terminology differentiating between instinctual and logical processing. *Goleman presents a theory on how our brain processes social interactions: The Low Road is our instinctual, emotion-based way we process interactions. It's how we read body-language, facial expressions and then formulate gut feelings about people.*

The High Road is our logical, critical thinking part of an interaction. We use the high road to communicate, tell stories and make connections

- She writes that there are "9 Social Intelligence Principles that Everyone Can Master"

1. Photo conversation, what is behind our words. Social Awareness and Social Facility: How you respond to others… Sensing other people's feeling… Knowing how to have smooth effective interactions. 2. Social triggers, being aware of how people and places trigger different emotions. 3. A secure place as discussed by Goleman. Everyone needs a secure place to recharge and process events and emotions. 4. Broken bonds which typifies a lack of empathy when people are treated as objects. This is discussed by Goleman. 5. Positively infectious, smiling truthfully engages others and creates a positive atmosphere quickly. 6. Adopt to adapt, taking the low road to understand the people around us and adapting accordingly. 7. Beware of the dark triad, the Machiavellian personalities that can be destructive. 8. Strive to be Mind Sight rather than Mind Blind. Mind Sight is about being able to guess what someone is going to say or what someone is going to do. Staying aware that self-absorption kills all empathy. 9. The People prescription is based on findings that those that have solid family and social relationships stay healthier longer, the message is to appreciate and nurture our relationships.

Structure - Charts

- http://creately.com/diagram-type/usage/decision-making-made-easy-creately - Decision Flow Charts

Strengths

Book on discovering strengths

- Rath, Tom, *Strengths Finder, Now Discover Your Strengths*, 2007.

Online discussions on strengths and weaknesses and SWOT analysis:

- https://study.com/academy/lesson/internal-strengths-weaknesses-in-swot-analysis-definition-examples-quiz.html

Strengths, Weaknesses, Opportunities, and Threats (SWOT) analysis implementation trough lessons in 30 topics.

- *https://yourbusiness.azcentral.com/organizational-strengths-examples-6556.html* by Sophie Johnson, 2018. Lists examples of gauging strengths by a company's functional areas.
- https://yourbusiness.azcentral.com/drawbacks-swot-analysis-8327.html , this describes the limitations of a SWOT analysis.

    A SWOT analysis does not provide a way to objectively compare and prioritize the factors that affect a business. Managers may have to rely on other planning tools, such as cost-benefit analyses, to judge which strengths, weaknesses, opportunities and threats are most important for a business to address. Consequently, a SWOT analysis may not be particularly useful by itself, but it can become more useful when combined with other strategic planning methods.

Success

Books on success:
- Halvorson, Heidi Grant, Ph.D., *Succeed: How We Can Reach Our Goals*, 2010.
- Niven, David, Ph.D., *The 100 Simple Secrets of Successful People, What Scientists Have Learned and How You Can Use It*, 2002.

Succession Planning

Books on succession planning
- Adamchik, Walter R., *Ensuring Leadership Continuity and Building Talent from Within*, Fourth Edition, 2010.
- Clutterbuck, David, Goldsmith, *The Talent Wave: Why Succession Planning Fails and What to Do About It*, 2012.

Online succession planning sources:
- https://assets.kpmg.com/content/dam/kpmg/pdf/2015/07/3468-succession.pdf, reference document on succession planning for family owned businesses, by Grant Walsh, 2011.
- http://iveycapitalgroup.ca/services/

    At some point every business owner will want to "exit" their business. Many times, however, the owner won't be able to leave voluntarily but will be forced to do so either due to incapacity or death. Without a proper business exit planning strategy, the involuntary loss of a key person can devastate a business by forcing liquidation during a chaotic time. Thus, proper exit planning should be an important part of a business owner's financial and estate plans.

- http://www.halogensoftware.com/blog/8-steps-for-effective-succession-planning
  Steps include establishing strengths, goals, objectives, succession plan and updating these at least once a year; preparing organizational charts and job descriptions; tallying talent and assembling appropriate talent pools; and defining stakeholder roles.
- https://www.ubs.com/microsites/together/en/will-i-be-missed-when-i-step-back.html
- Video by Robert Ettinger, Managing Director, Ettinger London, on taking over the family business. https://vimeo.com/138632840

Team Building

Book on team building:
- Harrington-Mackin, Deborah, The Team Building Tool Kit, Tips, Tactics, and Rules for Effective Workplace Teams, 1994.

Online discussion of team building with the Socratic method.
- http://www.ventureteambuilding.co.uk/the-philosophy-of-team-building-socratic-method/ About asking the right questions, by David Priestley, July 22, 2015.

  My way toward the truth is to ask the right questions." Socrates says in Plato's 'Protagoras' Socrates not only asked great questions, he also encouraged questions from others. Great questions get closer to the truth, and they also change attitudes. The aim of the Socratic method is to pursue the truth through constant analytical discussion.

Triple Bottom Line

Online discussion on the triple bottom line:
- http://www.cultivatingcapital.com/human-capital-people-triple-bottom-line/
  Human Capital –The "People" Part of the Triple Bottom Line, from newsletter by Cultivating Capital. Discusses the People, Planet, Profit approach to

the triple bottom line. The article discusses how and emphasis people relates to a sustainable organization. 2017.

Whole Brain Thinking –   Methodology and Coining Terminology
Whole brain thinking online discussions:
- http://www.wholebrainthinking.com.au/pdf/understanding_wb.pdf
  Copyright Dr. Kobus Neethling and Solutions finding (Pty) Ltd.
  Research documents at www.wholebrainthinking.com.au

  In the 1960's Philip Vogel and Joseph Bogen performed their breakthrough split-brain surgery on three epileptic patients. Roger Sperry (who received a Nobel Prize for this work in 1981) with his colleagues Bogen, Vogel and Gazziniga tested these patients and discovered that the two hemispheres control vastly different aspects of thought and action. They found the left (controlling the right side of the body) is dominant for language and speech and for analytical and logical thought, while the right (controlling the left side of the body) excels at visualizing, holistic and unstructured tasks. This breakthrough was followed by brain dominance research by Ned Herrmann, Jaquelyn Wonder Priscilla Donovan, Beverly Moore and others.

Wisdom from Philosophy and History
Greek philosophers on life, thought, ethics, and mindfulness:
- https://www.psychologytoday.com/us/blog/turning-straw-gold/201406/surprisingly-modern-wisdom-ancient-greeks-and-romans
  article from Psychology Today, Toni Bernhard, J.D., June 26, 2014.

  Socrates (circa 469—399 BCE) was a classical Greek philosopher and is considered one the founders of Western logic and philosophy. He established an ethical system based on human reason rather than theological doctrine. He maintained that the more we come to know ourselves, the greater will be our ability to reason and make choices that lead to true happiness.
  Quotations from Socrates:
  "Beware the barrenness of a busy life."
  "He is richest who is content with the least, for contentment is the wealth of nature."
  "The only true wisdom is in knowing you know nothing."

Plato (circa 428—348 BCE) was a Greek philosopher. Like Socrates, he is considered one of the founders of Western philosophy. He was a student of Socrates' and a mentor to Aristotle. He founded The Academy of Athens, which was the first institute of higher learning in the Western world. Quotations from Plato:

"The greatest wealth is to live content with little."

"Courage is knowing what not to fear."

"Necessity is the mother of invention."

"Ignorance is the root and stem of all evil."

Plutarch (circa 46—120 AD), Greek historian, biographer, and essayist. His famous work is a biography of Greek and Roman philosophers called Plutarch's Lives. Quotations include:

"Neither blame nor praise yourself."

"Painting is silent poetry, and poetry is painting that speaks."

"Know how to listen and you will profit even from those who talk badly."

- https://www.theguardian.com/sustainable-business/business-learn-from-ancient-philosophers - Guardian article on what we can learn from ancient philosophers, Jules Evans, May 4, 2012.

Socrates, one of the first philosophers, insisted on our right to think for ourselves… Aristotle based his ethics on a psychological theory of human nature, insisting that we are naturally virtuous, rational, social and happiness-seeking. Aristotle's philosophy was an influence on Edward Deci and Richard Ryan's Self-Determination Theory, which suggests that employees will work harder for you, and perform better, if you give them tasks they find meaningful and morally worthwhile…

Plutarch, understood that humans are incredibly social creatures, who constantly observe the people around them and imitate them… what you say to your employees is less important than what you do… If you talk about ethics and then cut corners at the first opportunity, they will follow your lead.

Epictetus coped with the insecurity of once being a slave by constantly reminding himself what he could control and what he couldn't. Focus on what you can control, and you will feel a measure of autonomy even in chaotic situations…

Musonius Rufus was known as the Socrates of Rome… If you want to be an ethical individual or an ethical company, you can't just study ethics, you have to practice it, every day, to get into good habits. The ancient Greek word for ethics is actually the same word for habit. We can keep track of this, for example by asking our employees (anonymously) how worthwhile they feel their job is. Then see if, in a year, we have managed to enhance their sense of purpose.

Epicurus was a fourth century Greek philosopher who taught, rather scandalously, that the aim of life was simply to be as happy as possible here on Earth… it could teach us how to bring our attention to the present moment, to savor it. Today, some companies are embracing Epicurus' philosophy, and trying to teach their employees the art of happiness.

Perhaps companies could create an ethical culture that embraces all these different ways of living.

Work Environment

Books on work environment from the standpoint of wellness.

- Chapman, Gary, *Rising above a Toxic Workplace, Taking Care of Yourself in an Unhealthy Environment*, 2014.
- Murphy, Shawn, *The Optimistic Workplace: Creating an Environment That Energizes Everyone,* 2015.
- Richards, Shola, *Making Work Work:* The Positivity Solution for Any Work Environment, 2016.
- Slaughter, Anne Marie, *Unfinished Business*, 2015.

Online sources on office space design trends

- http://www.officespacesoftware.com/top-office-design-trends-in-the-workplace-for-2016

    Key elements in office design address the expectations of millennials (and all team members) and make your office an attractive and productive workspace.

    A few principles: No more fixed layouts; Glass is the new wall; Green for efficiency; Clean, simple, decluttered; Zen principles on how environment affects work experience.

- http://workdesign.com/2015/03/how-to-apply-zen-principles-to-workplace-design/

Discussion on applying balanced principles to office design.

- http://www.nytimes.com/2016/02/28/magazine/the-post-cubicle-office-and-its-discontents.html?action=click&contentCollection=Magazine&module=RelatedCoverage&region=Marginalia&pgtype=article&_r=0

This article describes office design without cubicles and its advantages and disadvantages by NIKIL SAVAL, February 28, 2016.

Ultimately it's not clear whether the new offices work in the way they're advertised. Even when common spaces are covered over in beautiful, bright plywood paneling, as with Lenne in Tallinn, Estonia, the actual desks are often in open-plan setups. The move to take people out of private offices, the better to improve collaboration and productivity, has little empirical justification. Most widely cited studies of employee satisfaction tend to run against such trends in office design. A study from The Journal of Environmental Psychology in 2013 indicated that 50 percent of workers in open-plan spaces suffer from a lack of sound privacy, and 30 percent complain about a lack of visual privacy.

In 1980, the futurologist Alvin Toffler predicted that with increases in telecommuting technology, offices would soon become irrelevant. Downtowns would be emptied, and everyone would be connected through "electronic cottages" dispersed throughout the countryside. Digital advances in the years since have constantly threatened to make Toffler's fanciful vision a real one. It has come true in one sense: We do often work at home. But we also work at work, before going home to work more. Commuting and telecommuting exist in an unholy alliance. The office has persisted, becoming even bigger, weirder, stranger: a symbol of its outsize presence in our lives.

- https://www.linkedin.com/learning/improving-your-focus/protect-set-up-...

Course discusses the benefits of reinstating offices with doors for privacy and focus. Taught by Instructor - Dave Crenshaw - Keynote speaker and bestselling author on productive leadership.

In our hectic world, time management alone doesn't cut it. To truly increase your efficiency, it's crucial that you improve your focus as well as tend to your calendar. In this course, productivity expert and best-selling author Dave Crenshaw helps you develop the survival skills to both avoid daily distractions and stay focused on what's most valuable. Curate your digital and physical space to strengthen concentration, discover ways to keep your mind on task, and protect your relationships—both at work and at home—by focusing on what's most important.

Work Life Balance

Online discussion on work life balance:

- http://www.nytimes.com/2016/02/28/magazine/rethinking-the-work-life-equation.htm this article describes study about flexible schedules and productivity as well as employee health and happiness. By Susan Dominus, February 28, 2016.

    In the TOMO paper, half the employees in the technology department were randomly assigned to a control group, which would continue operating under the company's usual policy (flexibility given at the manager's discretion). The other technology employees would participate in what they thought was a new initiative but was, in fact, part of Moen and Kelly's field experiment. The new policy was both radical and, in concept, simple: Workers in the experimental group were told they could work wherever, and whenever, they chose so long as projects were completed on time and goals were met; the new emphasis would be on results rather than on the number of hours spent in the office. Managers were trained to be supportive of their employees' personal issues and were formally encouraged to open up about their own priorities outside work — an ill parent, or a child wanting her mom to watch her soccer games. Managers were given iPods that buzzed twice a day to remind them to think about the various ways they could support their employees as they managed their jobs and home lives.

    The research found that employees in the experimental group met their goals as reliably as those in the control group, and they were, in short, much happier: They were sleeping better, were healthier and experienced less stress. Other studies examining the same workplace found that the effects even cascaded down to employees' children, who reported less volatility around their own daily stresses; adolescents saw the quality of their sleep improve. A year out, and then three years out, employees in the experimental group reported less interest in leaving the organization than those in the control group.

ABOUT THE AUTHOR

Emma Kowalenko founded Kowalenko Consulting Group, Inc. (KCG) in 1988. Strategic planner, change management consultant, she has been documenting her clients' Organizational Health and Fitness (*OH&F*) throughout her career. Adjunct lecturer for Northwestern University, she produces course content, implements, and facilitates online Master of Science classes in the Executive Management for Design and Construction (EMDC) program, offered by the McCormick School's Department of Civil and Environmental Engineering.

Ms. Kowalenko is Lean Six Sigma Certified for Executives and Sponsors. Her mindfulness approach encourages engaging full brain thinking, creativity, and awareness of the subtleties of the multilingualism that surround us, professionally and socially.

The hands-on format in *Puliziotta's Organizational Health and Fitness (OH&F), Lessons Learned and Strategies for Zapping the DYSfunctional Virus*, gives you the opportunity to witness working lives touched by DYS and to participate in zapping DYSfunction. Here mindfulness practice and creativity are incorporated into DYS zapping techniques for public, private, and nonprofit sector clients. The tools in this book give you leadership competencies acquired through the interface of Emotional (EQ), Social (SQ), and Cultural (CQ) Intelligence.

Of eastern European heritage, Ms. Kowalenko born and raised in Casablanca, Morocco, emigrated to the U.S. at the age of 11. Fluent in six foreign languages, entrepreneur, small business advocate, oral historian, poet and mixed media visual artist, she is dedicated to giving visibility and voice to the unseen and the unheard.

KCG is located in Highland Park, Illinois. Ms. Kowalenko resides with her husband Anthony Bilotti in nearby Highwood, 28 miles from Chicago's downtown. Highwood is a diverse, creative, multi-ethnic, culinary-rich enclave, in close proximity to Lake Michigan.

All are invited to anonymously share ideas, working stories, *OH&F* challenges, and creative DYS zapping solutions on her blog / website www.puliziotta.com. Feel free to join her LinkedIn network.
https://www.linkedin.com/in/emma-kowalenko-84510012

56661682R00087

Made in the USA
Columbia, SC
30 April 2019